MURDER THY NEIGHBOR

For a complete list of books, visit JamesPatterson.com.

MURDER THY NEIGHBOR

TRUE-CRIME THRILLERS

JAMES PATTERSON

As seen on

GRAND CENTRAL
PUBLISHING

NEW YORK   BOSTON

Grand Central Publishing
Hachette Book Group
1290 Avenue of the Americas, New York, NY 10104
grandcentralpublishing.com
twitter.com/grandcentralpub

First Edition: September 2020

Grand Central Publishing is a division of Hachette Book Group, Inc. The Grand Central name and logo are trademarks of Hachette Book Group, Inc.

The Hachette Speakers Bureau provides a wide range of authors for speaking events. To find out more, go to hachettespeakersbureau.com or call (866) 376-6591.

ISBN 978-1-5387-5242-5 (paperback) / 978-1-5387-5241-8 (hardcover, library edition) / 978-1-5387-1896-4 (large print)

LCCN 2020937305

10 9 8 7 6 5 4 3 2 1

LSC-C

Printed in the United States of America

CONTENTS

MURDER THY NEIGHBOR

JAMES PATTERSON
with ANDREW BOURELLE

PART 1

CHAPTER 1

March 25, 1997

AT A QUARTER TO nine in the morning, Judge Stacy Moreno sits in her chambers at the Allegheny County Courthouse in Pittsburgh, reviewing the file of the case she is about to hear.

Moreno's office is austere, with no file out of place, no disorganized stack of papers to be seen. The shelves are lined with law books. The judge's robe hangs from a hook on the back of the door.

The case she is reviewing is an appeal of an earlier ruling.

Both the city's building and health departments have levied fine after fine against a homeowner named Roy Kirk, who bought one half of a row house in an up-and-coming neighborhood known as North Hills Estates, in the Oakland section of Pittsburgh. Apparently, the long-abandoned house needed a lot of work, but the work never got done. In fact, according to complaints from the neighbors, the house is in a greater state of disrepair now than when Kirk bought it.

A woman named Ann Hoover, who owns the adjoining house, has pushed again and again for the city to do something about the problem. She is scheduled to appear in court to testify against Kirk.

Hoover's property and Kirk's share a yard, a porch, and a roof. She is the most affected, but there are other neighbors involved, many claiming that Kirk's property is an eyesore that is bringing down the home values of the whole neighborhood. Judging from the photographs in the file, the judge can see why everyone is upset.

The place is a dump.

The siding is in desperate need of a paint job. Some of the windows are broken and boarded up. The roof is missing so many shingles that bare patches of plywood are clearly visible. And the lawn is not only overgrown with weeds, it's also full of garbage bags, as if Kirk has been using it as his own personal trash heap.

Kirk's appeal today claims that he is making a good-faith effort to restore the property, and that fines will only hinder his ability to get the work done.

Judge Moreno checks her watch and sees that it's 8:59. She rises from her cushioned chair and fastens her judge's robe around her. At nine o'clock on the dot, she steps through the door at the back of her chambers, which takes her directly to the raised bench overlooking the courtroom.

"All rise!" the bailiff announces. "The Honorable Judge Stacy Moreno now presiding."

Everyone in the courtroom rises.

"Thank you," Moreno says. "Please be seated."

From her elevated position, she can see everything in the courtroom clearly: the court reporter seated close to the bench, ready to take notes; the jury box, empty for the purposes of this hearing; the bailiff's dais, off to one side. The gallery is unusually full of spectators—presumably neighbors, all interested in the outcome of the hearing.

And front and center, of course, the tables where the plaintiffs and defendants—and their lawyers—are meant to sit.

A lawyer from the solicitor's office represents the city. But the lawyer for Roy Kirk sits alone. There's no sign of his client.

Kirk's lawyer rises, looking embarrassed, and asks if they can have a short recess as he tries to get in touch with his client.

"Your Honor," the assistant city solicitor interjects, "I support the motion for a short recess. Mr. Kirk's neighbor, Ann Hoover, is also not here. She is a key witness for the city."

Judge Moreno purses her lips, thinking. It's highly unusual for neither the defendant nor the key witness to show up.

"Aren't these two next-door neighbors?" she says.

A woman in the second row of the gallery stands up and catches the judge's attention.

"Your Honor, if I may," the woman says. "I live in the neighborhood. We went by Ann's home on the way to the courthouse this morning. We'd made arrangements to all come together."

She gestures to a man seated next to her—another neighbor, apparently—who nods his head in agreement. Both the man and the woman look concerned.

"There was no answer at her door," the woman continues. "I'm worried about her. I think something might have happened."

Judge Moreno thanks her and asks her to be seated. All eyes in the courtroom stare back at her.

"Bailiff," she says, turning to her longtime court official, "contact the Pittsburgh police and ask them to send someone to check on the whereabouts of Ann Hoover and Roy Kirk."

"Yes, Your Honor."

Judge Moreno turns back to the courtroom.

"Let's get to the bottom of this," she says. "Attorneys, please contact me in my chambers if you hear from either Mr. Kirk or Ms. Hoover. We'll be in recess until we hear something."

With that, she smacks her gavel down on its block, and the bailiff once again says, "All rise!"

Judge Moreno walks back to her chambers with a sinking feeling. She can't explain it, but she feels certain the courtroom will not be called back to order today.

CHAPTER 2

Ten months earlier

AS ANN HOOVER'S FINGERS dance over the keys of her Steinway piano, the notes of Chopin's Piano Sonata No. 2 float through her home. The hardwood floors and decorative brick walls make for good acoustics, one of the many things she loves about her house, where she's lived for the past decade.

She takes a break from playing, plucking her half-full wineglass off the smooth surface of the piano, and walks down the hall to the front of the house, then steps out on the porch to enjoy the sunset. The humidity of the day seems to be breaking, and the temperature isn't quite as suffocating as it's been. The warm glow of dusk fills the neighborhood.

Ann watches a teenage girl walking a dog, a man pedaling by on a bicycle, and a couple taking a stroll together, sharing an ice cream cone they bought down the street.

Ann loves this neighborhood.

The houses are affordable because most of them need some work. That was the case with hers. After she bought it, she had to put some serious effort into repairing it. As a capable single woman in her midthirties at the time, she did a little bit of the work herself—patching drywall, painting, even installing tile in the bathroom—but mainly she relied on friends or hired contractors to do the work. She learned a lot about what it takes to restore and maintain a house like this. It wasn't easy, but she loves the results.

The house is two stories tall, with additional space in the basement, and she's renovated and decorated it to be exactly the way she wants it.

There's only one thing she doesn't like about the house.

It's also the only thing she doesn't like about the neighborhood.

The house next door.

Ann's home is a row house, meaning it's half of a single building. When she purchased her property, it didn't look much different from the one next door. But there haven't been any buyers interested in the other side, which has continued to fall into disrepair. The FOR SALE sign sitting out front is hardly visible from all the weeds growing in front of it.

The house itself looks unappealing. Paint is flaking off all the exterior siding. The roof is full of bald spots where shingles have blown off in windstorms. The wooden supports holding the porch are rotten. Bricks have come loose from the foundation.

Just standing next to the place is spoiling her mood.

She takes her glass and heads back inside. She debates whether to crack open a new bottle and decides to indulge herself. She heads to the basement, where she keeps a small wine cabinet.

The wooden steps creak underfoot as she descends, and the temperature drops ten degrees, like she's walking into a cave. The basement is dark, with cobwebs hiding in the exposed floor joists above her. She hurries across the concrete floor to the cabinet, which abuts the brick foundation wall her home shares with the neighboring property. She plucks out a bottle of cabernet and heads back upstairs.

At the top of the stairs, she glances at a series of signatures written in permanent magic marker adorning the basement door. These were all the friends who helped her renovate the house after she bought it—she'd asked them to sign the door when she'd hosted a housewarming party after the work was finally finished.

After she pours herself a new glass, Ann walks back to the piano and sits down, her fingers poised over the keys. She takes a deep breath.

But as she's about to play the first notes, she stops herself. She cocks her head. Did she hear something?

She rises from her seat and heads back to the front door. She peeks out the sidelight and sees that a truck has pulled up in front of the neighboring property. A young man, probably in his midtwenties, is unloading tools from the truck bed.

She can't believe it.

She steps out onto the front porch as the man comes up the walk, holding a circular power saw in one hand and an extension cord in the other.

"Excuse me," she says. "Are you from the realtor's office?"

She's been trying to get them to repair the roof. The house needs work all over, but the roof is her main worry. She's afraid it might start leaking onto her side of the property, causing damage inside the walls.

"Nope," says the man, grinning broadly. "I own the place. I just bought it."

Ann can't help but smile.

"Oh, wonderful," she says. "I'm your new neighbor."

The man tucks the extension cord under his arm, freeing up his hand to offer it to Ann.

"Pleased to meet you," he says. "I'm Roy Kirk."

CHAPTER 3

I LOVE YOUR PLACE," Roy says to Ann, looking admiringly at her side of the row house. "I'm sure you're tired of living next to this eyesore," he adds, hooking his thumb to his own property.

"It just needs a little work," she says, downplaying it.

"Hopefully it won't be long before it looks as good as yours," Roy says.

They talk for a few minutes. Ann likes Roy right away. He's outgoing and energetic. Though he does seem a bit young to be tackling such a large renovation project, and she wonders if he really knows what he's getting himself into. Will he be so enthusiastic a month or two from now?

But Roy's big, innocent smile wins her over. She doesn't expect them to be best friends. After all, her forty-fourth birthday is just around the corner and she doubts he's even thirty yet. But Ann thinks they'll get along just fine, which is a relief to her. She's heard horror stories about bad neighbors in row houses.

Roy asks her what she does, and Ann explains that she works in marketing and gives piano lessons on the side.

"Music is my passion," she says. "I raise money for the Pittsburgh Symphony. You better be careful—I might hit you up for a donation."

Ann says it as a joke, and Roy laughs and pats his hand against the brick front of his home.

"Sorry," he says. "All my money is going into this baby."

"Of course," Ann says, smiling. "I definitely don't want to interfere with your renovations."

Ann asks what Roy does for a living, and he tells her that he has a home-repair business, which helps calm her fears about his being up to the renovation project.

"I used to deliver pizzas, but now I've got my contractor's license," he says, nodding toward his property. "The city's trying to get rid of its tax-delinquent houses. You can get places like this for dirt cheap."

Roy explains that he lives just down the street, and that he hasn't decided whether he'll move in here or sell this house after his renovations are complete. Ann can't help but feel a little disappointed. She's just met Roy, but he seems like he'd be a good neighbor. She hopes he doesn't end up selling the place to someone she won't like.

"This is a great neighborhood," Roy says. "So much potential."

"I couldn't have said it better myself," Ann says.

She tells him about the neighborhood association she's a part of, which has formed to help improve the area. So far they've held some community cleanups and a neighborhood yard sale, but there's been talk of trying to do more. The members want to organize community events, such as holiday parades, and find a way to build a promenade along the nearby Monongahela River. A community garden has been discussed. There are a few empty lots in the area that would make perfect locations for a public park, where they could hold picnics or other events.

Ann, who has a lot of experience with fund-raising through her work with the symphony, knows what a long shot it is to hope for some of the items on the group's wish list, but she's heartened by Roy's enthusiastic reaction.

"I bet in five years this neighborhood is going to be something special," Roy says.

He looks out at the twilight and says he better get to work. He wants to unload his equipment tonight before it gets dark. The house doesn't have any electricity.

"It was nice meeting you, Ann," he says, extending his hand again.

"It was a pleasure meeting you, Roy," Ann says, shaking it again. "Please let me know if there's anything I can do to help."

Ann walks back into her house. As she's sipping her wine, she feels happy. Roy seems like a friendly young man, and discussing the future of the neighborhood has left her excited. Her new neighbor's enthusiasm is infectious. She can't help but think of all the possibilities for the community around her—as well as for next door. It will be so nice to have that run-down place finally renovated. It's sat empty for so long that it hasn't always been easy for Ann to stay optimistic.

She sits back down to her piano and begins to play. But Ann's so excited, she can't concentrate. She heads back to the front door to tell Roy something that's occurred to her. Night is falling, and it's becoming too dark for him to work, but she catches him just as he's climbing into the cab of his truck. She shouts his name to stop him before he leaves, then hurries down the sidewalk. He rolls down his window and throws an elbow out.

"The neighborhood association is meeting next week," she tells him. "Would you like to come with me? I think it would be great if you could meet everyone else."

Roy smiles broadly.

"I'd like that a lot," he says.

CHAPTER 4

EVERYONE," ANN SAYS TO the dozen home-owners crammed into the small conference room, "I'd like you to meet my new neighbor, Roy Kirk."

Roy, seated next to her, rises and gives everyone a friendly wave. The attendees, a sampling of people living in North Hills Estates, all welcome Roy enthusiastically.

The neighborhood group is a mix of people, ranging from young homeowners to retirees, day laborers to lawyers. They have one thing in common—they love their neighborhood and want to see it thrive. Everyone present is on the board of trustees, but the meetings are rather informal conversations. The group currently has no president, no secretary, no treasurer. All the board members want to help improve the community, but no one can put in the time commitment needed to take the group to the next level.

"Roy," says Marjorie Wilson, whose property is just a

few houses down from Ann and Roy's, "tell us a little about what you've got in mind for your house."

"Total renovation," he says. "There's a lot of rotten wood inside. Some mold. I'm stripping everything down. The place is going to look like new."

As Roy talks, Ann can tell that the other members of the association are thrilled with what he has to say. They've all shared Ann's displeasure with the building standing vacant for so long.

"I actually have two houses in the neighborhood," Roy says. "Both on Lawn Street. I'm living in the other one right now, trying to fix them both up."

The conversation moves to a discussion about the neighborhood cleanup planned in a few weeks. As the hour-long meeting wraps up, everyone seems satisfied that they've accomplished a lot in their discussion.

"I only wish we could do more," Marjorie comments as an aside.

"Why don't we?" Roy asks.

Every head turns to Roy, who'd been silent during the earlier conversation.

"What do you have in mind?" asks Ted Fontana, a high school teacher who lives a few blocks away.

Roy leans forward, like someone who's been waiting for the right time to speak.

"Ann and I were talking," he says, "and it seems like there's so much more this association could do. I'm talking about community events that will bring everyone together. Easter egg hunt. Fourth of July barbecue. A trick-or-treat night on Halloween. At Christmastime, we could do an event with Santa. Families can come down, get some hot chocolate, get a picture taken with Santa and his elves."

"Come down where?" Ted asks. "That's the problem. We don't have anywhere to host these kinds of events."

"What we really need is a park," Ann says.

"Yes," Roy says, smacking his hand down on the table. "Why don't we work on getting a park?"

In the past, when the association discussed the idea, it had always been with a sense of defeat. *It's too bad we don't have a park.* But Roy's enthusiasm makes the others excited. Even Ann, who has always felt a park is a long shot, finds herself caught up in the zeal.

Ann offers to help find a property owner who might donate a plot of land for a community park. Soon the conversation has taken a new direction, how they need to recruit more members to the association so they can use the dues to build up a savings account.

"I think we're getting ahead of ourselves," Ted says. "We don't even have a president. I think that's the first step."

Ted's words have the effect of throwing cold water on a fire. Everyone is brought back down to earth, realizing that talking about all their lofty ambitions isn't the same as trying to put them into effect.

"I'll be the president," Roy says, smiling at the group.

"That would be fantastic," Marjorie says.

"Are you sure you know what you're getting into?" Ann asks Roy.

"Absolutely," he says. "I've got the time. I can do it."

Ann says she'd be happy to work with him to discuss fund-raising.

"I move that we make Roy Kirk president of the neighborhood association," Marjorie says.

"I second the motion," Ted says.

"All in favor?"

Everyone in the room raises their hand and says, "Aye!" It's unanimous.

CHAPTER 5

A FEW WEEKS LATER, Ann comes home from a morning walk to find Roy hard at work. His front door is hanging open, and the young man wrestles out a broken, water-stained sheet of drywall. He drags it down the porch steps and lays it on a growing stack, flattening the weeds. Before he turns to walk back into the house, Roy spots Ann approaching and offers her a bright smile.

"Making progress," he says.

His short hair is damp and beads of sweat stand out on his forehead.

Ann smiles at him and tells him to let her know if he needs anything.

"Maybe a glass of water," he says. "I forgot my water is shut off."

Ann is happy to do it. She walks into her house and takes a Tupperware cup out of her cupboard. As she's reaching into her ice tray, she can hear loud noises from next door—the sound of Roy ripping out more dry-wall. The sound stops for a moment and then, as she's turning from the freezer to the sink, a thunderous banging vibrates the room. The noise is so clear through the shared wall that it startles Ann, and she almost drops the water cup. As the banging continues, she collects herself and runs the tap until the water turns cold.

What on earth is Roy doing next door?

After filling the cup, she lets herself into Roy's house. The front hall is filled with tools and equipment: hammers, saws, boxes of nails. The only light comes from the windows. As she steps deeper into the hallway, it becomes harder to see. What light is available is so bright, it makes the shadows even darker. She stubs her toe on a broken piece of two-by-four lying on the floor.

The noise, she realizes, is coming from upstairs. She climbs the dark corridor, her feet crunching dirt and debris. When she makes it to what she assumes is the bedroom—the house's layout mirrors her own—she finds Roy bathed in sunlight. He swings a sledgehammer against the studs in a wall already stripped of its Sheetrock. The board breaks free of its nails and dangles from the ceiling. He repositions the hammer and takes a wild swing, knocking the two-by-four free. It clatters against the floor, joining a handful of others. Nails jut out of each end of the board, like some kind of medieval weapon.

"Oh, thanks," Roy says, noticing Ann standing a safe distance from the doorway.

"Are you sure that's not a load-bearing wall?" Ann says, pointing to the wall he is currently disassembling.

"I'm sure," he says, taking a drink.

The room is in disarray, with hunks of drywall piled in the corner on top of a mound of pink insulation, which looks wet and spotted with black stains. The state of the house is worse than she realized—much worse than her house when she first moved in. The walls are water-damaged, the boards rotting, the plaster falling off in clumps. The room feels dank, and even though the window is open, there's a strong smell, like socks that have been left in a gym bag for too long.

"I know," Roy says, without Ann needing to say anything. "I've got my work cut out for me, don't I?"

Ann offers him a sympathetic smile.

"I know good contractors," she says. "Want me to give you some numbers?"

"Nah," he says, waving his hand dismissively. "I'm going to do everything myself. It will take longer, but I'll save money."

"You know how to do all this?" she says, gesturing to the mess around him.

"What I don't, I'll figure out," he says. "Can't be that hard, right?"

Ann doesn't answer. When it came to renovating her home, there was so much she didn't know.

Does Roy realize what he's gotten himself into?

CHAPTER 6

ROY THANKS ANN FOR the glass of water. Before she leaves, she hesitates. She's been wanting to talk to him about something, but she isn't sure if now is the right time. She takes a deep breath.

If not now, when?

"Let me ask you something," she says. "Can you come out onto the porch with me?"

He follows, taking a drink as he walks. Out on the porch, Ann points to the wooden railing that runs around the perimeter—half on her property, half on his. The paint has long since flaked off and the handrail and the balusters are rotting. A few have come loose from the railing and lean at uneven angles.

"I've gotten a quote to replace all of these porch railings," Ann explains, hoping Roy will be okay with what she has to say. "To do it right, we really need to replace all the wood at once."

This is one of the last pieces of work she wants to do on her property. She's waited until now because she needs the consent of the next-door owner to do it.

"It will look like crap if it's only on one side," she says. "All the wood should match."

"Let me take care of it," he says. "I'll save us both some money."

Ann was afraid he would say this. On the list of repairs Roy needs to make on his side of the property, fixing the porch railing can't be a high priority. Judging by how slowly he seems to be making progress on his own side—he's only there one or two days a week—she doubts he would get to it anytime soon.

"I'd really love to have this taken care of," she says. "And I've seen the work this guy does. It's fabulous. If you're okay with it, I'm willing to pay for your half."

"I couldn't let you do that," Roy says, looking around, as if thinking about what the work would entail.

Ann feels nervous; she likes Roy, but she doesn't want to give in and let him do the work. She hasn't seen any of his craftsmanship yet—only his demolition—but he doesn't strike her as capable of professional-level work. And she thinks the quote she's been given is very reasonable.

She doesn't want to get into a fight with her new neighbor, though.

"Let's just put the idea on hold," Ann says. "You've got

bigger jobs on your to-do list. And this porch has looked like crap for a while now. It can wait a little longer."

Roy looks around again.

"I'll tell you what," he says. "You go ahead and get your contractor to do the work. I'll pay half. It's a good idea. It will make the place look better while I concentrate on more important things."

"You sure?" Ann says, relieved.

"Yeah," he says, nodding. "Who knows when I'll get to it anyway."

"Thanks," she says. "I really appreciate this."

"We're neighbors," he says. "We're in this together."

CHAPTER 7

ONE MORNING IN MIDSUMMER Ann is sitting on the porch, drinking a cup of coffee and admiring the craftsmanship of the new railing and balusters, when Roy pulls up in his pickup truck. It's the first time he's been back since she had the work on their porch done.

Seeing him pull up, she has a moment of panic. She has a crazy thought that he'll forget he consented to the work. Or that he'll object to not having given input on what it would look like. Or that he'll find some problem with the craftsmanship.

"Wow," he says as he comes up the walk. "This looks great!"

Ann smiles, relieved, and invites him to sit down. She's been anxious to talk to him about his plans for the homeowners' association. The next meeting is coming up, and she'd like to at least show up being able to say that she and Roy have discussed a plan of how to proceed.

But Roy declines her invitation to sit. He says he has work to do.

"I'm sorry I've been MIA," he says. "I've been tied up with other things. I'm trying to buy another house."

"Another one?" Ann says, unable to hide her surprise.

"Yeah. It's not far from here."

"You sure you can handle three houses?" Ann asks, wishing he would focus on repairing the houses he already has before buying another.

"Actually," he tells her, smiling sheepishly, "this will be eight."

"Eight!" Ann exclaims, her eyes going wide.

He shrugs, as if it's no big deal. "They're so run-down that the prices are a steal," he says. "I got one for less than two thousand bucks. This one," he adds, gesturing to the property adjoining Ann's home, "was only sixty-eight hundred."

Right, Ann thinks, *but the reason they're all so cheap is because they need a lot of work.* Having seen the inside of Roy's property, she can only guess how much it's going to cost him to fix it up. The house might have been inexpensive, but the renovations won't be.

Roy doesn't appear concerned. He seems his usual enthusiastic, unflappable self.

He walks down to his truck and hauls a bundle of long extension cords from the passenger seat. He drops the end of one coil in the front yard and then begins to walk down the sidewalk, unspooling it as he goes. "Just going to run this down to my other house so I can use the electricity," he explains to Ann.

He doesn't ask Ann if he can plug the extension cord into one of her outlets, which would certainly be easier than linking several cords and running them down the block. She considers making the offer, but refrains. She wants to be neighborly, but she's afraid if she gives an inch, he'll end up taking a mile. Would he expect to use her electricity whenever he was making repairs? Would he want to use it even when she wasn't home?

She likes Roy. She does. He seems like a nice guy who means well. But so far she's been unimpressed with his ability to actually get anything done.

A few minutes later, Roy comes walking up the sidewalk again, smiling. He doesn't seem to be bothered in the least that she didn't offer to let him use her outlet. He takes a few tools out of his truck—a hammer, a level, a chalk line—and carries them into the house. He comes back out a moment later and starts unloading sheets of plywood from the bed of his truck. He wrestles the sheets one by one through the front door.

Again, Ann thinks about offering to help, but this isn't the kind of work she's used to doing. She can paint and patch drywall, but carrying a four-by-eight board that probably weighs forty pounds is exactly the type of thing that she hired professionals to do.

A few minutes after Roy gets the last sheet inside the

house, the circular saw fires up, carrying its squealing sound outside.

So much for her peaceful morning on the porch.

But Ann isn't irritated. In fact, she couldn't be happier that Roy has started working again.

As she heads into her house, it occurs to her that Roy never mentioned paying her back for the work on his side of the porch. She wonders if she'll ever see that money. As long as Roy fixes his side of the row house into something halfway decent, she decides, she won't press him about the payment.

It seems like a small price to pay to finally have the house next door looking livable.

CHAPTER 8

WHAT A STORM," Ann remarks. She's on the phone with her neighbor, Marjorie Wilson, and cradles the receiver in the crook of her neck as she pulls back the curtain to look outside.

Rain pours down in thick streaks, shimmering in the light from the streetlamps. The roadway is a stream of water, and as a car drives by, it sends waves into the air on both sides.

"Forecasters are predicting rain all week," Marjorie tells her.

Ann's downspout gushes water, creating a small pond in her front yard. On Roy's side of the porch, where there are no rain gutters, the water falls from the roof in sheets. His yard is full of junk—garbage bags, piles of broken two-by-fours, the Sheetrock he ripped out months ago—and all of it is getting soaked.

Ann says, "We'll be lucky if we don't lose elect—"

Before she can finish the sentence, lightning flashes and thunder cracks so loudly that she flinches, almost dropping the receiver.

"Wow!" Marjorie says. "That one made me jump."

Ann walks into her kitchen. She switches the cordless telephone to her other ear and begins tidying up. She wipes the counter down and puts the dishes in the drying rack away.

Marjorie changes the subject from the weather to the reason she called.

"Do you know if the association is meeting this week?" Marjorie asks.

Ann takes a deep, exasperated breath. "I have no idea," she says.

Roy canceled the last meeting, and there's been no word yet if the next scheduled meeting is going to happen. Because Ann is Roy's neighbor—and she's the one who brought him to that first meeting—everyone keeps asking her for updates, as if she's become his personal secretary. Her enthusiasm over him becoming president four months ago has long since abated.

"I say we meet with or without Roy," Ann says. "We didn't have a president before. So what if our president isn't around now?"

"Do you think he'll be mad if we meet without him?"

"How can he be mad?" Ann says. "He hasn't done anything as president. Does he expect us to sit around and wait for him?"

Ann doesn't say what she's really thinking, that having Roy as president has actually been worse than having no one at all. Before, someone would step up and do the work. Things got done. Now that everyone assumes Roy will take care of things, nothing ever gets done.

"I'm sure Roy's busy," Marjorie says. "He's got eight houses, after all."

"I just wish he'd focus on one thing and get it done," Ann says, thinking specifically of the house next door.

"Has he been working on the house at all?" Marjorie asks.

"He's over there all the time now," she says, "but doesn't seem to be getting anywhere fast."

It's true—Roy is often next door. She sees his truck parked out front, and she'll hear the occasional banging noise or whine of a power saw. One day he showed up hefting a new porcelain toilet into the house. Another day he had a bundle of bricks delivered to the front yard, which he has yet to touch. He set two bags of cement next to the stack, leaving them out in the elements to get rained on. They must be hard as rocks by now.

Most days she sees his truck, yet she hears nothing coming from next door.

"I don't know what he's doing over there," Ann says. "He's spent all this time tearing out wet and rotting wood, but I bet this storm is soaking everything all over again."

"I feel bad for the guy," Marjorie says.

"Me, too," Ann says. "I think he's in over his head and just doesn't want to admit it. But if the guy can afford to buy eight houses, he should be able to afford to hire a contractor to do the work for him."

After they hang up, Ann decides to make it an early night. It's the kind of miserable weather that begs a person to climb into bed, get cozy, and read a good book before drifting off to sleep.

Upstairs, the sound of the rain is louder, pummeling the roof. She walks to the corner to turn on her bed-side lamp.

She yelps when her feet step in cold water.

"What the...?"

A puddle the size of her kitchen table is growing on her hardwood floor. A drip falls from the ceiling and splashes into the puddle with a soft *plop*. She stares at the ceiling. Sure enough, a wet spot close to the wall that she shares with Roy is discernible in the plaster.

Her roof is practically brand-new. It's Roy's roof that looks like a dog with mange. The water must be leaking in from his side and pooling atop the ceiling, spreading over to her side.

Her heart pounding, she picks up the phone in her bedroom. She tells herself to remain calm. *Be polite. Don't let Roy know how angry you are about this.*

But he doesn't pick up the phone, and she's unable to leave a message, either.

"Damn it, Roy!"

She stomps downstairs and grabs a pan from the kitchen and a beach towel from her linen closet. She mops up the puddle and places the pan under the drip.

As the water *pings* into the pan over and over, she can't sleep. Her mind races, and she can feel her blood pressure rising.

She wishes Roy Kirk had never bought the house next door.

CHAPTER 9

THE NEXT MORNING, ANN peeks out her front window and sees Roy's truck sitting at the curb. She steps out onto the porch. The gutters have finally emptied, but the grass and pavement are still wet. The air is cold, but there's a hint of blue breaking through the gray sky.

The familiar extension cord runs up the wet sidewalk and into Roy's front door, ajar as always.

Ann knocks on the door. When there's no answer, she pokes her head inside.

The one previous time she was in the house, when Roy began working, she thought it was in disrepair—but it looks ten times worse now. The hallway is cluttered with both construction debris and tools, so jumbled together that she wonders how he can keep track of them all.

She hears some kind of rustling noise upstairs.

"Roy!" she calls out, trying to make her voice sound as friendly as possible. "Are you home?"

"Who is it?" Roy says, his voice not particularly friendly.

"It's Ann," she says. There's a pause, and she has the weird feeling that maybe he's forgotten her name. "Your neighbor," she adds.

"Be right down," he says.

She hears the clatter of some kind of tool—it sounds like he threw it down—and then his feet clomp down the stairs. He emerges from the darkness so quickly that she wonders if he's hurrying because he doesn't want her to walk into the house.

She steps back out onto the porch, and a second later he joins her, closing the door behind him as much as he can with the cord in the way.

"Sorry," he says, smiling. "I'm just trying to clean up some water. The storm made a mess of things last night."

"I know," she says. "That's why I'm here."

"You've got a leak, too?" he asks, his voice so innocent and naive that she momentarily feels bad for what she's about to say to him.

"No," she says. "The leak is coming from *your* side of the roof."

"How do you know?"

Her patience snaps.

"My roof is practically new, Roy. Yours is the one missing shingles. Anyone walking by the house can take one look at your roof and know it's going to leak."

Roy looks up as if he can see through the porch ceiling, with an expression on his face as if it's never occurred to him to work on the roof. Ann's frustration with Roy has been brewing for a long time, and she decides not to hold back now.

It's time to give him a piece of her mind.

"Roy," she says, "the roof is the first thing you should be working on. You're spending all this time ripping out water-damaged wood inside. Well, where do you think the water is coming from?"

"It's not all coming from the roof," Roy says. "Some of it's coming through the walls, too."

Ann stares at him, dumbfounded. *So fix that, too!* she wants to shout.

Instead, she says, as calmly as she can manage, "Look, I know you want to do all these repairs yourself, but you need to hire some help. I have the number of a good roofer. Get someone to fix your roof right away. Then you can take your time doing whatever it is you're doing inside."

"Take my time?" he says, giving her a sharp look. "I'm sorry if I'm not moving fast enough for you."

Ann ignores the comment.

"I'll get you my guy's number," she says. "He can probably come over today, put some tarps up there to stop the worst of it, and then reroof the whole house as soon as the weather breaks. It's going to rain again tonight, you know."

"I've got some tarps," Roy says. "I'll go up there and do some triage."

"Do you have a ladder that can get you on the roof?" Ann asks, astounded that she feels the need to ask such a question of someone who claims to be a contractor.

"It might reach," he says, stepping to the edge of the porch and looking from the grass to the porch roof.

"Roy," she says, stepping out into the yard and pointing toward the roof. "The leak is on the second floor. You need a ladder to get up there."

"I know, Ann. I'm not stupid."

He steps out into the yard with her, looks up at the second story of their row house.

"I'll take care of it, okay?" With that, he stomps up the porch steps.

"Thank you," she says, trying to sound genuine but sure she's coming across as pushy.

As Roy steps into his place, he tries to slam the door behind him, but the door won't close because of the extension cord in the way. It bounces back open and he grunts in frustration, trying to force the door shut, but again, the cord won't let it latch.

Finally, he storms away, leaving the door hanging open a few inches.

CHAPTER 10

NOT LONG AFTER, ANN sees that Roy's truck is gone. She assumes he's headed to the hardware store to purchase an extension ladder and some tarps. She tries to play her piano, but she can't concentrate. She paces, checking and rechecking the front window for any sign of Roy.

Three hours go by, and still there's no sign of her neighbor.

The clouds in the sky start to darken again, building toward another storm. The forecasters are predicting another gully washer.

Ann has the sinking suspicion that Roy isn't going to return. She paces the house, unsure what to do. Then she gets an idea—two, in fact.

First, she picks up her cordless phone and takes it to her office. She looks through her file folder with all the receipts and invoices from the work she had done on her house, and dials the roofer who installed her roof. She explains who she is, reminds him that he did her roof, and explains that she has a leak.

"I don't think it's my roof," she assures him. "I think it's coming from my neighbor's. I just want you to come over and check it out to make sure."

She wants to have documentation from a professional showing that the problem isn't on her side.

The roofer says he doesn't mind checking, since he wants to ensure she's happy with the work he did on her roof, but it'll be a few days before he can make it over— his plate is full after last night's storm.

Ann agrees, and after she hangs up, she puts her second idea into effect.

She goes into the storage closet in her office and roots around. A minute later, she pulls out her Canon camera. She hasn't used it in a while and is worried she doesn't have any film, but she checks and finds one roll. She'll have to buy more if this problem with Roy continues, but one roll should be enough for what she has in mind today.

She steps outside and begins snapping photos of the trash filling Roy's yard, and the broken, boarded-up windows. She crosses the street to get a photo of the entire property. She tries to zoom in on the roof on Roy's side, but she's not shooting from the best vantage point. She goes inside and calls a neighbor, Phil, whose property backs up against theirs.

"I know this sounds like a weird request," she says, "but can I take a photo from your second-story window?"

When she explains what she's doing, Phil says, "Be my guest. I'm tired of looking at that dump. I can't tell if it's a house or a landfill."

From Phil's bedroom window, she has a good angle on the roof, both her side and Roy's. She takes plenty of photos, but she makes sure to leave a few frames on the roll.

She stays for a few minutes to chat with Phil, but when she notices raindrops starting to fall onto the sidewalk, she hurries home. The sprinkling turns heavier, and soon after she gets in the door, the sky opens up and unleashes another deluge onto Pittsburgh.

Ann watches from her front window as the rain pours down.

There's still no sign of Roy.

Tonight, she's prepared. She takes a pan upstairs, positions it back in the spot where she had it last night. An hour later, the *ping, ping, ping* of water begins to sing through the room.

The ceiling plaster has turned a shade of gray from the saturation.

Ann points her camera at the wet spot.

Click.

PART 2

CHAPTER 11

October 1996

REBECCA PORTMAN WALKS DOWN Lawn Street to Roy Kirk's residence—not the property next to Ann Hoover's house, the place down the street where he actually lives. She is a petite woman in her early thirties, with curly brown hair and freckles on her nose and cheeks. She wears a black trench coat and carries an umbrella to shield her from the rain that's just begun.

It's dusk, and the sky is full of black, menacing clouds. The light rain she's walking through is only the beginning—a real storm is only minutes, if not seconds, away.

When she knocks on the door, Roy answers almost immediately, beaming at her.

"Hello, beautiful," he says.

This comment brings an electric smile to Rebecca's face—a smile that Roy says is what made him fall in love with her.

She's never met anyone quite like him before. When they started dating a year ago, she wasn't sure what to make of him at first. He was sweet, kind, attentive. Not like the guys she usually went for.

Not long after she and Roy started dating, Rebecca had a little too much to drink one night and showed up at her ex-boyfriend Bill's house to tell the jerk she'd found someone who finally treated her right. Bill called the police on her, and she ended up in the drunk tank. She sat in the cell, worried sick she'd blown it with Roy, but he surprised her by arriving with bail money and an understanding smile. She'd expected an angry, judgmental reaction, but he simply told her everyone makes mistakes.

She realized just how much he cared about her. Two months later, when he dropped down on one knee to propose during an evening walk along the Allegheny River, she said yes.

She hasn't regretted the decision, although she's been reluctant to take him up on his offer to move in together. As much as she loves Roy, Rebecca doesn't particularly like coming over to his house.

His front hallway is lined with animal cages filled with mice, hamsters, and other rodents. The air smells of the wood chips that line the bottoms of the cages. The animals squeak and squirm, and she averts her eyes so she doesn't have to look at them. Otherwise, the place is nice. Roy doesn't own much, but what he has he takes care of well. The living room is neat and orderly. He even keeps his bathroom clean—which, in her experience, is unheard of for a man living alone.

But the thing he keeps in the upstairs bathroom?

Just the thought of it makes her shudder.

Roy and Rebecca head to the kitchen, where Roy is making them dinner. He moves about the kitchen as he moves about life—full of energy. He never sits still. He stirs the spaghetti sauce, adds spice, starts the noodles boiling, all while asking her how her day was, taking her coat, pouring her a glass of wine.

"How's the work going on the houses?" she asks, hoping for good news.

His mood changes at her question.

"Everything's going fine," he says, but his words don't sound convincing. "I just have a lot to do."

She notices that he doesn't quite look himself. The way he bounced around the kitchen had distracted her at first, but there's definitely something wrong. He looks tired, like he's not getting enough sleep.

"Can I help?" she says. "I don't mind getting my hands dirty."

"No, no, no," he says. "I want to surprise you when the house is ready."

She isn't sure which house he means. He's driven her past most of them, but she's only been inside a couple.

As they're sitting down to eat, the phone starts ringing.

He doesn't answer it. And since he has no answering machine, it just rings and rings.

"Aren't you going to get that?"

"No," he says. "I'm sure it's just my pain-in-the-ass neighbor."

"Why would she be calling? I thought you two got along. You did that porch thing together."

He rolls his eyes and smirks.

"Her roof is leaking, and she thinks it's coming from my side. Don't worry. I'll take care of it."

Rebecca tells Roy that he needs to be more mindful of his neighbor's feelings.

"Don't close off communication with her," Rebecca says. "You still have to live next to her."

"I don't live there."

"*We* could live there someday," Rebecca says.

"Fine," Roy says. "I won't ignore her."

As if on cue, the telephone rings again. Roy looks at it hanging from the kitchen wall, and his expression makes it clear that answering it is the last thing he wants to do.

"Fine," Rebecca says, standing. "I'll do it."

Before Roy can stop her, Rebecca snatches the phone out of the cradle and says hello. She listens for a moment and then says, "May I tell him who's calling?" She covers the receiver and whispers to Roy, "It's Henry from the neighborhood association."

Roy frowns and takes the phone. Rebecca sits back

down and watches Roy on the phone while she picks at her food. She only gets his half of the conversation.

"No...I haven't looked at it yet...you're kidding?" And then after a long period of silence on Roy's end, he says, "Thanks for letting me know."

When he hangs up the phone, he is quiet for a moment.

"That bitch!" he finally snaps, so violently that Rebecca recoils.

"What happened?" Rebecca asks, concerned.

"That woman," he says, angrier than Rebecca has ever seen him, "you won't believe what she's trying to do."

CHAPTER 12

THANK YOU ALL FOR COMING," Ann says to the neighborhood association board. "I've called this meeting today to consider a motion of no confidence in our president."

Ann stares out at the members of the association, letting her eyes linger for an extra few seconds on Roy. His expression—scared, hurt—reminds her just how young he is. He's wearing a shirt and tie for the occasion, but the shirt clearly hasn't been ironed.

He seems like a nervous wreck, and she actually feels sorry for him.

But he's brought this on himself. If he's in over his head, it's irresponsible of her—and the board—to keep enabling him.

"As you all know," Ann says, "since Roy took over the presidency, we've accomplished virtually nothing as a community association. All his big talk has turned out to be just that—*talk*."

The mood in the room is far different tonight than when she first brought Roy to a board meeting. Then, everyone was all smiles, full of hope and admiration for their new young, energetic neighbor. Now the mood is grave. Every face staring at her is silent.

Ann clasps her hands in her lap to keep them from shaking.

"But even worse than his ineffectiveness on this board, the state of disrepair of his own home exemplifies exactly what this board stands *against*."

Ann opens a manila file folder in front of her and passes around eight-by-eleven photographs she's taken of Roy's property. The pictures emphasize the bricks missing from the foundation, the flaking paint on the siding, the holes in the roof. Really, it's the garbage in the front yard that's the most disturbing. Without the trash, his house might look like just another abandoned building. With the trash, it looks much worse.

Her fellow board members examine the photos with interest, even though most of them have seen the house themselves.

This is their neighborhood, after all.

"Since Roy bought the property on Lawn Street," Ann says, "the state of disrepair has actually worsened. His front yard has become his own personal junkyard, which is the opposite of the ideals we want to put forth with this association."

Roy's stare burns into her. Gone is the hurt boy. The person glowering at her is an angry, frightening man.

Ann softens her tone, not necessarily because of his glare. This was her planned rhetorical move all along: first, be harsh—then be compassionate.

"I like Roy," she says. "We all do. He's a nice guy. He means well. But he clearly has too much on his plate. He can't give the time to the presidency that the position needs. If we remove him from the presidency, that's one less thing for him to worry about."

She says that maybe Roy can focus his attention on his home renovations and get his houses looking like something he—and the rest of the community—can be proud of.

"This is what's best for the board," Ann says, "but it's also what's best for Roy."

Henry, an electrician who lives a few blocks away from Ann, turns to Roy and says, "I'd like to hear from Roy. Maybe we don't have to do a vote of no confidence. If this is what he wants, he could simply resign."

Every face in the room turns to Roy, whose incensed expression has reverted back to that of a wounded, sad young man.

"Thank you," he says, and rises from his chair to address the room. "I appreciate the opportunity to defend myself against this outrageous attack from Ann Hoover, who has proven time and again that she has a personal vendetta against me."

CHAPTER 13

ANN FEELS A CHILL at Roy's words.

Outrageous attack?

Personal vendetta?

The guy is an irresponsible homeowner who has turned his front yard into his own private scrap heap. And he thinks *her* actions are the ones that are outrageous?

"I will not resign," Roy says from the start. "If you don't want me as your president, you'll have to vote me out."

After this, Roy begins a long speech. He admits that he has neglected his duties as president of the association. However, he explains, the big plans he has for the community will take time. He can't get immediate results overnight. He has been working on the group's bylaws, he says, which he thought would be the best first step for the group.

"As for my own house, the one on Lawn Street next to Ann's, I've turned a corner on the renovations," he claims. "I really think things will start to move much quicker. Sure, the place looks rough now, but that's what it takes to make improvements. Sometimes you've got to tear a thing down before you can build it back up."

Ann rolls her eyes, but the others are rapt. Roy can be so charming that Ann fears his words are having an effect on the board.

"Let's talk about what this really is," Roy says, leveling his eyes on Ann. "Character assassination."

Her breath catches in her throat.

"Ann isn't satisfied with my progress on the Lawn Street property," he says. "As soon as I bought the house, she was riding me about fixing the front porch when I had other things I should have been dealing with. But I tried to be a good neighbor and went along with what she wanted."

Ann is fuming. *He* tried to be a good neighbor?

"This isn't the right venue for Ann's grievances," Roy says. "What happens at my property has nothing to do with this association. She's trying to punish me with this passive-aggressive attack."

"That's not true," Ann replies, barely able to control her trembling voice. "This association exists to help beautify the neighborhood. Your house is the biggest black mark in the neighborhood. As president, you should be the model for other residents. Instead, you're the model of what *not* to do."

"I own eight properties," Roy says. "All of them are in various states of renovation. But you don't see any of my other neighbors in here complaining about me. You're the only one being unreasonable."

"Maybe *those* roofs aren't leaking and causing water damage to the neighboring properties," Ann snaps. "Maybe you're not using *those* yards as landfill. Do you take garbage from your other houses and dump it in the yard on Lawn Street? You're certainly not doing enough work on the house to accumulate that much trash!"

Roy leans over, clenching his teeth and pointing toward the table, as if ready to shout at Ann. But before he can say anything, Ted Fontana speaks up and says, "All right, all right. We've heard from both Roy and Ann. Does anyone else want to say anything before we vote?"

The association members look around, everyone too timid to speak up.

Finally, Marjorie Wilson says, "I'm going to vote to have Roy removed."

She turns to Roy and says she's sorry.

"I like you, Roy. I wish you the best in all your projects. I really do. But Ann's right. You need to focus on your own properties. I hope someday we can welcome you back to this association."

"Marjorie's right," Ted says. "You focus on your own homes—let us focus on the neighborhood."

The others speak up and concur with Marjorie and Ted—they all want Roy to know there are no hard feelings but that they think this is what's best for everyone.

"All in favor of removing Roy Kirk as president?"

"Aye," they all say, though no one says the word emphatically.

Even Ann feels sad, rather than pleased—she can't believe it's come to this. But hopefully, this will serve as a wake-up call for Roy.

"Sorry, Roy," Ted says.

Roy doesn't respond. He walks out the door without a word. There seems to be a collective sigh of relief in the air.

After the meeting, as people are milling about chatting, Marjorie finds Ann, who is still shaken.

"You okay?" Marjorie says.

"Did you hear him?" Ann says, upset. "Passive-aggressive attack? Not the right venue?"

"It's okay," Marjorie says. "You got what you wanted. Calm down."

"I'll tell you what," Ann says, "if he doesn't make some serious progress on that property—fast—he's going to be sorry."

"What are you talking about?"

"If he wants me to go to the right venue to air my grievances," Ann says, "I'll call the city housing inspector."

"Ann," Marjorie says, trying to calm her friend. "You have to live next to this guy—try not to go to war with him."

But Ann doesn't seem to be listening.

"Passive-aggressive? *Humph*. He doesn't want to see me aggressive-aggressive."

CHAPTER 14

USE THE BLACK KEYS to tell you where you are on the piano," Ann instructs Jody, her nine-year-old piano student. "That's what they're there for."

"Okay," the girl says, orienting her fingers into place.

"Ready to start again?"

Jody begins to play Beethoven's "Für Elise," a good song for beginners. The notes ring through the house beautifully.

Bang! Bang! Bang!

The cacophony from Roy's house next door breaks Jody's concentration, and the little girl stops, exasperated.

It's annoying, but Ann can't be mad at Roy. The truth is she *wants* him working. Hopefully, if he's over there making noise it means he's one step closer to finishing his renovations.

"Try not to get distracted," Ann tells Jody. "Think of this as good practice for when you're giving a recital.

You can't control the noise the audience makes. Talking. Coughing. Sneezing. You have to concentrate on what you're doing, not the noises around you. You should be able to play even if the sky is falling."

Jody positions her hands again, ready to begin. Another sound interrupts her—this time it's a soft knock at the front door.

"Your mom's here," Ann says.

When Ann opens the door, Jody's mom, Jennifer, gives Ann a hug. They visit for a few minutes on the front porch, catching up. When Jennifer was Jody's age, Ann used to babysit her and give her piano lessons. The two have kept in touch on and off ever since. So when Jody expressed interest in learning to play the piano, Jennifer knew just who to call.

"Sometimes when I'm sitting next to Jody at the piano," Ann says, "I get this feeling of déjà vu, like I've gone back in time and it's you sitting next to me at the piano."

Jennifer laughs. As they talk, more banging comes from inside the house next door.

Jennifer comments on the growing garbage pile in Roy's front yard.

"I know," Ann says, shaking her head in embarrassment. "At least he's working."

Roy has been there erratically since being kicked off the neighborhood association board a month ago. Ann had worried that he might retaliate by refusing to work, but the opposite was true, at least for a while. At first he tackled the work with what seemed like renewed vigor. But, as always, Ann has trouble seeing any real progress. It's unclear exactly what he is doing. More garbage bags have appeared in the front yard, while building supplies are now occupying Roy's side of the porch. There's a stack of two-by-fours and a box of drywall nails. There is also a single bundle of shingles. Ann has no idea what he plans to do with them—the whole roof needs to be reshingled. One bundle won't do much good. Her roofer confirmed as much when he came to check her roof. He said Roy's place must be leaking like a sieve, and he even took some photographs for Ann while he was up there.

The weather has been cold in Pittsburgh for the past month, but today has been unseasonably warm— one last Indian summer day before winter really sets in. But the warmer weather has also revealed a new problem: an odor emanating from the garbage in Roy's front yard.

Ann wants to move the conversation into the house, but Jennifer says she and Jody need to run. As they turn toward the street, the nine-year-old shrieks, "Look, Mom!"

Ann follows Jody's finger and also finds herself gasping.

They all watch as a rat—its black fur wet and scruffy— crawls out of a hole in one of the garbage bags. It pushes between two other bags and its pink tail disappears out of sight.

"Ann," Jennifer says, facing her old babysitter, "this is

disgusting. I'm sorry, but I can't bring Jody back here until that place is cleaned up."

Ann is speechless, still in shock herself. She feels like she suddenly needs a shower.

Where there's one rat, there have to be more.

And these rats could get into *her* house!

As Jennifer and Jody drive away, Ann stomps over to Roy's front door and begins pounding as hard as she can.

"Get out here, Roy! Right now!"

CHAPTER 15

ROY OPENS THE DOOR a crack and sneers, "What do you want?"

He looks terrible—his eyes are bloodshot, his hair is growing long and needs to be brushed, and it looks like he hasn't shaved in a couple weeks. He doesn't step out, and the door isn't open far enough for Ann to look inside. All she can see behind him is darkness. There's no sign of the extension cord, and it doesn't appear that the electricity is working, either.

How can you work in the dark? Ann thinks.

She points to the trash heap in his yard and says, "There are rats. You have to get this garbage out of here."

Roy smirks, annoyed. He steps out of the house and closes the door behind him. Close up, Ann can see that his hands are filthy, and an unpleasant odor emanates from his body, as if he's gone as long without a shower as he has without a shave.

He steps around his two-by-four pile and looks at the yard.

"Are you sure?" he says. "Maybe it was a stray cat."

"I know the difference between a rat and a cat, Roy!"

Roy turns on her, his eyes flaring with anger.

"Take it easy, Ann. You're always getting so mad about everything."

"Take it easy?" she repeats, dumbfounded.

"Relax," he says. "And mind your own business."

Ann's blood is boiling.

"This *is* my business, Roy," she says, her voice shaking. "You still haven't fixed the roof. Every time it rains, the water leaks over into my house. I just lost a piano client today because she doesn't want to bring her daughter to a house next to a scrapyard crawling with rats."

"You're overreacting," Roy says, going back inside. "Let's agree to just leave each other alone. I won't bother you if you won't bother me."

With that, he slams his door shut. He throws the deadbolt loudly.

Ann can't believe it. She is shaking.

She stews over his words. *I won't bother you if you won't bother me.* She's a good neighbor—she's never given him any reason to bother her!

Ann storms into her house, slamming her own door.

"I've had it," she says out loud, virtually in tears.

She goes to the phone book, flips to the section with the numbers for city officials, and places the call.

"Hello," she says into the receiver. "I'd like to talk to the city housing inspector."

CHAPTER 16

ROY'S FIANCÉE, REBECCA PORTMAN, knocks on his front door. She takes a moment to look behind her at the rain just beginning to fall. When there's no answer, she knocks harder. Finally, Roy comes to the door, looking surprised to see her, then his expression quickly turns to a dawning realization.

"Hey," he says. "Sorry. I totally forgot you were coming over."

He opens the door, and she is greeted by the familiar smell of wood chips. But there's another odor, too, an unpleasant one. As she walks through the front hallway, she quickly figures out what it is. Although Roy is ordinarily really good about cleaning the animal cages, keeping the feces buildup to a minimum, now the cages are full of droppings. The mice and hamsters are crawling around in their own waste.

The rest of the house is messier than usual, too. Roy

is ordinarily fastidious about keeping everything in its proper place, but tonight she sees shoes and clothes lying around the living room, along with a handful of balled-up fast-food wrappers on the coffee table and a couple issues of *Playboy* lying on the floor. She's surprised to see them out; she knows Roy owns some adult magazines, but he usually keeps them hidden when she's around.

"Are you okay, Roy?" Rebecca asks, genuinely concerned.

In a moment of vulnerability, Roy once told her that he'd spent time in a psychiatric hospital as a teenager for being what he simply called "obsessive-compulsive." He said he'd been fine since then, and she'd never noticed any problems or had any complaints—besides, of course, all the animals.

"I'm fine," he says, plopping onto the couch. "Just a little stressed is all. I told you that woman, Ann, got me kicked off the neighborhood association, right? Well, now she's got the city housing authority on me. I've got an inspection tomorrow."

Rebecca sits down next to him on the couch and places a comforting hand on his knee.

"I keep getting crank phone calls," he says. "All hours of the night, the phone rings like crazy. I finally took it off the hook."

That explains why I only got a busy signal when I tried to confirm our dinner tonight, Rebecca thinks.

"She's turned the whole neighborhood against me," he complains. "Someone threw a firebomb at the house."

"A firecracker?"

"No. A bomb. A Molotov cocktail. I had to put it out with a fire extinguisher."

"Did you call the cops?"

"Yeah, I told them my neighbors are harassing me, but they just told me I need to work it out with them."

Roy throws his head back and rubs his eyes. He looks terrible. And now that she's sitting next to him, she can't help noticing that he has an odor to him as well. How long has it been since he took a shower?

"Please let me talk to this woman," Rebecca says. "I bet I can help smooth things out."

"No," he says, shaking his head. "It's too late for that."

He is quiet for a moment, and all Rebecca can hear is the sound of the rodents squeaking in their cages. Most of the cages are in the hallway, but there are several in the living room as well. She notices something in one that makes her skin crawl.

"Jesus, Roy, is that one dead?"

They both approach a metal cage full of mice. One of the mice—with white fur and a red nose—lies on its side in the wood chips. A fly is crawling on its face.

"Damn," Roy mutters. "I guess I forgot to feed these guys."

Rebecca feels sick to her stomach.

"Speaking of feeding," he says nonchalantly, "I bet the beast is hungry."

"Can't that wait until I leave?" Rebecca says.

"I don't want her to starve," Roy says, as if another hour or two would make a difference.

He pulls back the door at the top of the cage and reaches into the squirming mob of mice. They writhe in a frenzied mass as he dips his fingers into the pile. A second later, he lifts a live mouse by its tail.

The little white mouse flails about like a fish hanging from a hook. He carries it through the house, twisting and kicking. Rebecca doesn't usually like to watch this, but she follows Roy upstairs anyway.

He opens the bathroom door and pulls back the shower curtain. Inside a claw-footed tub lies an eight-foot python, its head bigger than her fist, its shiny skin a yellow color blotted with patches of reddish tan.

"Hello, beautiful," Roy says to the snake, and Rebecca feels ill when she realizes it's the same greeting he gives her.

He lowers the mouse into the tub. It tries to scurry up the side of the porcelain, but it can't get a grip and keeps sliding back down. The snake, moving patiently, starts slithering toward the tiny mouse.

As the python approaches its prey, Rebecca stares at its cold, reptilian eyes. She averts her gaze and finds herself instead looking at Roy's face. He stares down at what's about to happen with the same cold detachment as the snake slithering toward its victim.

"Roy," Rebecca says, her breathing shallow. "I've gotta go."

"Okay," he says, without looking away.

It's as if he's caught in a trance.

Rebecca hurries from the house, almost in a run. The screeching of the mice in the hallway seems to follow her out into the street. She forgot her umbrella but doesn't go back to get it. The cold rain actually feels good against her hot, clammy skin.

Partway down the block, she stops and puts her hand on a street sign to steady her trembling legs. She gulps in air, quelling the panic attack threatening to overtake her.

When she's finally calmed her nerves, she looks up and realizes she's right in front of Roy's other house, the one that's been such a source of trouble.

All it takes is a glance at the row house—the siding coming off, the boarded windows, the pile of garbage bags in the yard—and she finds herself agreeing with the woman who lives next door. Any reasonable person would want Roy to do something about the place.

What the hell is happening to my fiancé? she thinks.

CHAPTER 17

ANN PEEKS OUT HER front window.

Roy stands in his yard in the bright sunlight, talking to a man wearing a tie and holding a clipboard. The man had pulled up in a van with CITY OF PITTSBURGH stenciled on the door. Ann can't hear what they're saying.

The man points to the garbage and construction debris in the yard, the black bags beaded with water from last night's rain. Roy scratches his head, looking sheepish. Next, Roy escorts the man into the house. They're in there for what feels like an excruciatingly long time. Finally, Ann hears the men talking in the backyard, and she peeks through another curtain at them chatting outside.

Roy is all smiles—the same charismatic guy who'd charmed the neighborhood board when she first introduced him.

Ann doesn't like the idea of eavesdropping, but she leans in close to the window to try to hear.

"I know who ratted me out," Roy says jokingly.

"We got a call about the property," the inspector says. "I can tell you that, but I can't say who it was from."

"Oh, I know that," Roy says, jovial. "But I know it's my neighbor over here. You can assure her that I'll be getting all of this taken care of right away. She doesn't have anything to worry about."

The inspector makes a few more notes on his clipboard, then he pulls off a sheet of paper and hands it to Roy.

"Thanks for helping me out today," Roy says, still grinning. "I learned a lot about building code."

The two shake hands, and they walk around the side of the house toward the front. Ann hurries down the hall and looks out the front window.

Roy walks the inspector to his vehicle and waves as he drives away. As soon as the van is gone, the mask on Roy's face—the friendly, likable young-man mask—disappears and is replaced by someone angry as hell.

He heads right for her door.

"Oh, no," Ann whispers and retreats into her house.

Roy begins pounding on her door, much as she'd done to his before.

"I know you're in there!" Roy practically shouts. "I know you ratted me out!"

Ann feels the compulsion to hide, but she doesn't want to back down to Roy—she's in the right here, damn it!

She opens the door but doesn't step outside.

Roy takes the piece of paper in his hand and shakes it in front of her face.

"I hope you're happy," he says. "I have to appear in housing court now. And he's going to send the city health inspector out here, too."

"It's not my fault," Ann snaps, pointing to the garbage in front of the house. "You've got rats, Roy. I've seen more and more of them."

"They're going to fine me, you know," he says, his tone going from angry to exasperated. "I don't have this kind of money to just throw away."

He steps away from the door and heads to the edge of the porch. Ann interprets this as an invitation to step outside. She doesn't want to, but she decides to anyway.

"I'm doing the best I can here," Roy says, his tone now one of desperation. "This is just going to set me back. Can you just get off my back and let me finish the work?"

"All I want is for you to finish," Ann says, her exasperation matching his. "I want that more than anyone. Probably more than you."

"This is my dream project," Roy says. "I'm going to finish if it kills me."

"Roy," Ann says, trying to take as calm a tone as possible. "It's time for you to get some help. You can still do a lot of the work, but you need to get some professionals here to help you."

"I can't afford that," he says. "All my money is tied up in these houses."

"Then sell one of them," she says. "Sell all of them."

"The idea of flipping houses is to make a profit," he says. "I can't get what I paid for this. I need to fix it up before I can sell it."

Ann feels a pang of sympathy. It's obvious Roy's taken on more than he can actually handle, and he can't see a way out. But clearly the answer isn't to continue what he's been doing.

"I just wish you'd get off my back," Roy says.

"I'm not being unreasonable," Ann says. "No one would want to live next to this."

Roy glares at her again. It's eerie how quickly his expressions can change—how he can look like a help-less, hapless boy one second, then an angry, intimidating man the next.

"Leave me alone, Ann," Roy says, flinging his front door open. "Or you'll be sorry."

He doesn't slam his door. He shuts it calmly, as if they'd just had an ordinary conversation. The calm-ness is almost worse; it feels more calculated, which is especially unsettling considering he just threatened her.

Ann stares at his door, trembling, before finally walk-ing back into her house. She paces down her hallway, sits down at her piano, tries to play. Then she realizes she doesn't want to be in her house—doesn't feel safe in it—and grabs her keys and leaves.

Down the street, out of sight of her home, she

leans against a brick building and puts her head in her hands.

She sobs.

She doesn't know what to do, what her next step is. She hates that her home, the place where she once felt more at peace than any other place in the world, is no longer her sanctuary.

She wipes her tears away, tries to collect herself. This isn't who she is. She feels a growing sense of resolve. She's no pushover.

If Roy Kirk wants a war, she'll give him one.

CHAPTER 18

THANK YOU ALL FOR coming on such short notice."

Ann stands before the neighborhood association board. It's mid-January, and one of her New Year's resolutions was to address the problem with her neighbor head-on. No more messing around. She's not going to spend another eight months waiting for him to finally do something.

"I want you all to know," she says, "that Roy Kirk is scheduled to appear in housing court. He is facing hefty fines from both the city housing department and the health department. I am here today," she adds, "to ask if you'll join me in testifying against him."

The board members look around at each other, murmuring their surprise. Luckily, this time Roy isn't in the room, glaring at her. But she's just as nervous as she was when she pushed for the vote of no confidence.

"Ann," Henry says, "I'm not sure this is the appropriate venue."

"There's a blight in our neighborhood," Ann says, "and the man responsible refuses to do anything about it. This affects all of us."

Most people look skeptical, but Marjorie Wilson speaks up, saying she knows someone in the area trying to sell their home.

"They were shocked when the assessor came and valued their house at less than expected," Marjorie tells the group. "When they asked what was wrong, the assessor told them plain and simple, 'It's that house down the street—the one with all the garbage in the yard.'"

Several people in the room look stunned, wondering what this means for their own home values.

"It's called external obsolescence," Ann explains. "That's when factors outside of your property can affect its value. I talked to a lawyer and he says our property values—all of our property values—could be as much as 10 percent lower as a result of Roy Kirk's dereliction. His other properties could be having the same effect."

"But what good is going to court going to do?" Henry asks. "I don't want to make life harder for the guy."

"That's the other thing," Ann says. "I plan to file an injunction that will compel him to fix the problem."

"A lawsuit?" Henry asks.

"Yes," Ann says. "And I'd like you all to join me as co-plaintiffs."

Henry shakes his head, suggesting Ann is going too far. But others don't look so uncertain—they want something done about Roy's property almost as much as Ann does.

"My lawyer explained that there are three steps you should take when in a dispute like this," Ann says.

The first, she says, is to try to work it out with your neighbor.

"I've tried that, and it hasn't done any good."

The second step is to notify the city to enforce its codes. She's tried that, too, but so far Roy hasn't addressed any of the building and health inspectors' concerns.

"Filing a lawsuit should be the last resort," Ann says. "But I'm sorry to say I—we—have arrived at the last resort. It's clear that Roy Kirk is not going to fix up his house on Lawn Street unless he's forced to do so."

Ann explains the logistics of the suit—who her lawyer is, how to join the suit, the timeline for filing, potential outcomes. And even if people don't want to join, she encourages them to still attend the court hearing and testify about what they've witnessed regarding Roy's property.

Marjorie says she'll join. Ted Fontana also agrees. So do a few more, though others are on the fence. Some are adamant that they want no part in it.

"I like Roy," says Frannie, a restaurateur who lives on the opposite side of the community, most likely out of harm's way from Roy's property value–draining eyesore. "I can't do this to him."

"I think you're making a big mistake," Henry says of the lawsuit. "Just give him time and let him do the work."

"There are rats in my yard, crawling under my porch," Ann retorts. "How long should I wait? Until the rats come in my front door and sit down at my dinner table?"

Henry shakes his head.

"I sympathize with you," he says. "I understand you're frustrated. But this is only going to make matters worse. I don't think anything good will come of this."

CHAPTER 19

ANN PACES AROUND HER apartment. All of the paperwork is in order to file the lawsuit, but she's asked her lawyer to wait a few days.

She has one last idea before going that far.

She tells herself that she needs to stop worrying and get it over with. She pulls on her winter coat, steps out onto the porch, and knocks gently on Roy's door. The air is cold, and a light frost covers the trash heap in Roy's yard.

"Roy," she says, trying to sound unconfrontational. "Are you there? I'd like to talk to you."

Roy's truck is parked out front, but she hasn't heard him working. No extension cord runs to the door, even though there is still no electricity inside.

"I don't want to fight. I just want to—"

The door opens so fast that Ann steps back.

"What do you want?" Roy says, squinting like a person

who's just stepped out of a dark movie theater into bright sunlight.

"I want to talk to you," she says, "about...our situation."

"Our situation?"

It looks like it's been months since Roy last cut his hair, and his stubble has grown into a bushy beard.

"Please, Roy. Just come out onto the porch and listen to what I have to say."

Roy takes a deep breath and steps outside. He's not wearing a shirt or shoes—a shocking sight in the middle of February. His chest is pale and thin, his ribs clearly visible, his stomach practically pinned to the back of his spine. His pants look two sizes too big and are held up by a leather belt pulled tight around his emaciated frame. His face looks gaunt, his eyes red.

Ann backs away, genuinely afraid of him. Where is the charming young man she met last spring? This zombie in front of her cannot be that same person.

Ann has the sick feeling that Roy's just been sitting in the darkness inside his home.

Not working.

Not eating.

Just staring into the dark.

She tells herself she has to give it a try. She won't feel right about suing if she doesn't at least make the offer.

"Roy," she says. "I have a proposition for you. I'd like to buy your house."

Roy tilts his head and looks at her sideways, as if trying to figure out if this is some kind of joke.

"Clearly you've taken on more than you can handle in buying this place," she says. "You can just walk away from it. Let me worry about fixing it up."

Roy says nothing, so Ann goes on, explaining that she's talked to a real estate agent and her bank. She can get a loan that would allow her to purchase the house for what Roy paid and also allow her to make the renovations it needs.

"You won't lose any money," she says. "I'll give you what you paid."

She thought this might please him. Roy must feel trapped. Unable to finish the renovations. Unable to sell the house in the state it's in. There's no way he could get what he paid for the place from anyone else—not with the disrepair it's in now.

She's giving him a way out.

The *only* way out, as far as she can tell.

But Roy doesn't seem to think of it that way. His eyes narrow, and he glares at her.

"What about all the work I put into it?" he asks. "The time and money—how do I get that back?"

Ann feels helpless. If he can't see that she's offering him a key to the prison he's locked himself in, she doesn't know what to do.

"I can't pay more than what you paid," Ann says. "The bank loan wouldn't just be for purchasing your house— I'll need some money to fix it up."

Roy smirks as if he can't believe what he's hearing.

"This is a good deal for you, Roy. Let me take this place off your hands."

"Is this what you've wanted all along?" he sneers. "You've been hassling me from the start to try to get my place for a steal?"

Ann shakes her head, frustrated.

"I don't *want* your house, Roy. I want *you* to take care of it. But you're not doing it, so I feel like I have to."

"Whatever," Roy says.

"Please consider it," Ann says. "You'll be able to wash your hands of this place. This is your last chance."

As soon as she says it, Ann regrets her choice of words.

"Last chance?" Roy says, scrutinizing her face. "Or what?"

Ann doesn't want to tell him, but she feels it will be worse if he's blindsided when he receives the legal paperwork.

"I'm going to file an injunction against you," Ann says.

"An injunction? What's that mean?"

"I'm about to sue you, Roy," Ann snaps, her patience at its limit. "I can't figure out any other way to get you to fix this damn place up!"

Roy looks truly frightening. With his greasy hair, unkempt beard, and shirtless bony body, he looks more like someone who's just stepped off Charles Manson's commune than the pleasant young man who first bought the house next door nine months ago.

"Let me tell you something," Roy snarls, his yellow

teeth clenched like a growling animal's. "Fixing up this house is my dream. My dream. You will not stop me."

Ann looks at him sympathetically.

"I'm sorry, Roy. It's time to find a new dream."

With that, she walks into her residence. She hears him slam his door so hard it rattles the windows on her side of the property. A loud cacophony comes through the walls—boards falling, tools flying.

She pictures him inside, working himself into a rage.

In the dark.

CHAPTER 20

ANN SITS WITH MARJORIE and Ted in the second row of the courtroom. In front of them, the assistant solicitor sits in preparation for making the city's case against Roy. Ann has talked to the city's lawyer in anticipation of testifying today. He's going to give her time to present all the information she has about Roy's negligent homeownership.

At the other table sits a lawyer whom Ann assumes Roy hired.

So far, there's no sign of Roy.

Ann is ready. She has a file folder in her lap with photos of Roy's house and documentation of her interactions with the city's building inspectors.

"Where is he?" Marjorie asks, checking her watch and turning to look at the door at the back of the courtroom.

Several people from the neighborhood are in attendance—some to testify, some to support Ann, and some just curious about what will happen. But as the clock ticks down the minutes to the nine o'clock hearing, Roy still doesn't appear.

It would be just like him not to show up, Ann thinks. After all, it's not as if he's shown much interest in obeying the law when it comes to maintaining and renovating his home. She can picture him having the same disregard for an order to appear in court.

"What happens if he doesn't show?" Marjorie asks, keeping her voice low in the hushed courtroom. "Will they issue a warrant for his arrest?"

Ann opens her mouth to say she doesn't know what the consequences will be, but there's no need to answer—the door to the courtroom opens and in comes Roy Kirk.

Ann is surprised to see him hobble forward on crutches, with a bright white bandage wrapped around the top of his skull.

She notices that his dress pants are stretched out around one of his thighs as if there's a bandage or a brace underneath.

"What the heck happened to him?" Marjorie whispers.

Ann has no answer. She can only stare as her neighbor hobbles down the aisle to sit next to his lawyer.

As soon as he's seated, the bailiff announces, "All rise!"

Roy struggles to his feet with the rest of the people in the courtroom. He winces as if in pain as they sit back down and the judge addresses the courtroom.

"Mr. Kirk," says Judge Walter Martinez, with a puzzled

expression on his face, "may I ask what happened to you?"

"I've been shot, Your Honor," Roy says. "Twice. Once in the leg and once in the head."

Ann and Marjorie exchange surprised looks.

"Did the police arrest who did it?" Judge Martinez asks.

"I can't go to the police," Roy says. "I don't trust them."

The judge makes a sour face.

"Mr. Kirk," he says, "if you've been shot, you need to speak to the police."

Roy doesn't say anything.

Ann watches in disbelief. *What the hell is going on?*

Judge Martinez asks if Roy feels okay to continue the hearing, and Roy says that he does not want a delay.

"I want to get everything out in the open," he says. "Clear the air."

The judge explains that the city solicitor is going to call witnesses to testify about the condition of the house on Lawn Street, but the hearing can begin with a statement by Roy, if he wants to make one.

"I do, Your Honor," Roy says, rising and using his crutches to balance on one foot.

"You may remain seated, if you like," the judge says.

"I want to stand, Your Honor. I want to stand up to the way I've been treated. By my neighbors and by this city."

Roy starts in on a diatribe about how he's been shunned by his community. How Ann Hoover has turned his neighbors against him. How his house has been vandalized.

"People have thrown firebombs at my house," he says.

Ann and Marjorie exchange another puzzled look.

"Is this the house next to Ann Hoover?" Judge Martinez asks. "Or down the street, where you live?"

"Where I live. But it's because of Ann Hoover's harassment that this is happening. I don't know who attacked me—who shot me—but I'm sure it's related."

Roy looks visibly shaken, his voice trembling. Even without the apparent physical injury, he looks completely stressed-out and mentally exhausted.

Ann can't be sure if he's telling the truth or if his behavior is an act. She knows Roy well enough now to realize that he's capable of emotional manipulation. But while it's true that several neighbors are mad at Roy for the condition of his house, Ann can't believe anyone would vandalize his house or throw Molotov cocktails, or whatever he means by "firebombs," at his house. And if Roy's been shot, there's no way anyone in the neighborhood had anything to do with it.

She doesn't want to believe he would lie about being shot, or having his house vandalized, but at this point, she wouldn't be surprised if the bandages were part of an elaborate hoax.

Still, while her gut tells her that the injuries might be fake, everything else she's seeing from Roy—his haggard appearance—seems real.

The judge says that he's very sorry that Roy has gone through these ordeals. However, he adds, this is not the venue to address those claims. If Roy has been vandalized and attacked, he needs to seek help from the police.

"This hearing is only to address your property and whether or not you've adhered to building and health codes. Understand?"

"Yes, sir," Roy says, sitting back down and muttering, "I just want you to know the whole neighborhood has turned against me."

Judge Martinez then shifts his attention to the solicitor.

"I'd like to call my first witness," the lawyer says. "Ann Hoover."

Ann takes a deep breath. She tries to put Roy's crazy claims out of her mind. She needs to focus.

This is her chance to get something done about the leaking, rat-infested dump she's been forced to live next to.

CHAPTER 21

HOURS LATER, ANN HOOVER sits in the gallery of the courtroom, waiting for the judge to return after a thirty-minute recess.

She's hungry, tired, and anxious. They've been in court all day. She testified. Marjorie Wilson testified. Other neighbors testified. The city solicitor brought in real estate experts to talk about the negative effect Roy Kirk's place has had on neighborhood property values. He brought in the city housing inspector to talk about the ways in which Roy's property is out of compliance. He did the same with a representative from the health department. Finally, he showed the judge the photographs Ann has taken over the past several months, including one from just a few days ago, showing a cluster of rats digging into a garbage bag in Roy's weed-filled yard.

Roy's lawyer tried to rattle some of the witnesses—

he asked Ann why she was *harassing* Roy—but for the most part he was unable to offer much defense as to why his client's home looked worse now than when he bought it.

Through it all, Roy sat at the defendant's table, impassive and hardly moving.

Judge Martinez is a fiftysomething man with a salt-and-pepper beard and a barrel chest. Throughout the hearing, Ann has been impressed by his no-nonsense, get-down-to-business demeanor.

"I've considered all the evidence," the judge says, his booming voice matching his appearance, "and I've reached my decision."

Ann's heart accelerates. Her breathing feels shallow.

"There is a preponderance of evidence," Judge Martinez says, "that you, Roy Kirk, have been derelict in your duties as a homeowner."

Relief floods through Ann.

"Your neighbors, specifically Ann Hoover, have done their due diligence in trying to get you to clean up and repair your property. She has asked you, encouraged you, and offered to provide you with the contact information for professionals who could help."

Ann risks a glance over at Roy, who seems like he's watching a TV show that he finds particularly boring, not even looking at the judge deciding his fate.

"In recent weeks," Judge Martinez continues, "your house has undergone various inspections, and it has failed them all miserably. By all accounts, you have done nothing to remedy the problems."

Ann can't believe it. The judge's words feel like a vindication of everything she's been saying since Roy moved in.

Yes! she thinks. *Let him have it, Judge!*

"Roy Kirk," the judge continues, "this court hereby fines you in the amount of fifty thousand dollars."

Ann's mouth drops open.

She hadn't expected *that* kind of penalty.

Once again, Ann feels sorry for Roy. She knows he can't afford this. If he had fifty thousand dollars lying around, surely he would have put it into the house.

"Moreover," Judge Martinez says, "I am hereby stripping you of your building license. I can't have someone who so brazenly disobeys building laws and health codes operate as a licensed contractor in this city."

Ann hears murmurs from the neighbors around her.

Judge Martinez goes on to outline a tight schedule for Roy to comply with Pittsburgh's codes. If he doesn't, he could incur more fines. As the judge explains the situation, the courtroom is as silent as a cemetery.

It feels nothing like the court scenes Ann's seen in movies, where, once the verdict is stated, there are cheers and celebration in the audience.

There's nothing to celebrate here. There's nothing to feel good about.

Ann feels a surge of anger. Roy pushed her into this mess.

What was she supposed to do, just sit around and let him turn his property—and by association, her property—into a pigsty? She shouldn't have to feel guilty.

After the judge disappears through the door behind his bench, the room relaxes a bit. Roy huddles with his lawyer. If he's upset, he's hiding it well. Marjorie gives Ann a hug. Ted does, too.

"That's a big fine," Marjorie comments. "And how's he supposed to do the work if he doesn't have a building license?"

"He'll need to hire someone," Ted says, "which is what he should have done in the first place."

As they talk, Roy rises from his seat and, without a word, hobbles out of the courtroom on his crutches. Marjorie and Ted talk, but Ann's distracted when she sees Roy's lawyer motion for the city solicitor to approach.

The two chat for a minute, looking more like old pals than adversaries. The solicitor walks back over to her.

"This isn't over," he tells Ann. "Roy's going to appeal."

"What does that mean?" Ann asks.

He explains that Roy might do some work on the house, clean up some of the mess. That way, when they go to appellate court to discuss the appeal, Roy will be able to argue that he's making an effort to address the issues and that the fines should be reduced or even waived.

"I'd be okay with that," Ann says. "I don't want to bankrupt the guy. I just want him to finish what he started."

"We'll see what happens," the lawyer says. "Maybe this was the wake-up call he needed."

Ann remembers thinking the same thing when they kicked him off the housing board.

How many wake-up calls does one guy need?

CHAPTER 22

REBECCA PORTMAN POUNDS ON Roy Kirk's front door.

"Roy, it's me!" she yells. "Answer the door, damn it!"

She hears footsteps coming, and then from the other side of the door, Roy hollers, "Go home, Rebecca! It's not safe here for you."

Go home?

No way.

He won't answer his phone. She doesn't even know if their engagement is on or off—frankly, she's not sure she *wants* to marry him anymore. But she still cares about him, and wants to make sure he's okay.

"I'm not leaving until you open this door," she says. "Do you understand me?"

After a short pause, Roy finally says, "All right. Hold on."

But instead of opening the door, he walks away,

deeper into the house. She balls her fist to hammer the door again, but then hears Roy coming back down the hall.

He opens the door quickly, and she gasps when she sees a bandage wrapped around his head.

"Roy, what the . . . ?"

Roy steps out on the porch and shuts the door behind him. Rebecca is stunned—why won't he let her inside?

And why is he wearing a bandage on his head? His bushy hair sticks out around it like those old pictures of tennis player John McEnroe wearing a headband over his long hair.

Roy goes over to the porch railing and leans against it. He's wearing sweatpants, and it looks like there's something bulky underneath the fabric on one of his thighs. He seems to be in serious pain.

"What's going on?" Rebecca asks. "I wanted to know how the court hearing went."

"Terrible," he says, pointing to his skull. "And someone shot me."

"My God," she says, her heart racing. "Did you go to the hospital? Did you call the police? Why didn't you call me?"

Roy tells her it's not safe for her to be over. The whole neighborhood has turned against him and is trying to drive him away.

"What did the police say?"

"I can't go to the police," he says. "They're on her side."

Rebecca is at a loss for words. *What is going on?*

Roy changes to a more soothing tone. He tells her not to worry. An appeal is scheduled, and he's going to make all the repairs by then. The judge will rescind the fines, and everything will go back to normal.

"And then we can get married," he says. "But first I have to fix this."

"Let's go inside," she says.

"I can't let you in. It's too dangerous here."

"If it's not safe here, you should come to my place," she says. "Let me help you."

"I have to do this alone," Roy says, and reaches to embrace her.

Rebecca falls into his arms, unsure what to make of what Roy's saying. She remembers how understanding he was when he bailed her out of jail, how supportive he was. He was there for her in exactly the way she needed.

She tells herself that she needs to be there for him, too.

If she can do that for him, and if he can fix the mess he's gotten himself into, maybe there's hope for them yet.

"I love you, Roy," she says.

"I love you, too."

As Rebecca walks toward her car, parked a few houses down, she turns and sees Roy still standing on the porch. He lifts his hand and gives her a wave.

She waves back.

He blows her a kiss.

She blows one back to him, then keeps walking. When she arrives at her car, she looks again to the house, expecting him to still be standing there. But the porch is empty, the light off. Later on, she'll remember this moment.

The way he blew her that good-bye kiss.

And then was gone.

PART 3

CHAPTER 23

March 24, 1997

ANN SITS AT HER piano, her fingers moving over the keys. The notes reverberate around her, filling her home with the beauty of Chopin on a rainy night. It's after dinner—later than she would normally play—but she's trying to keep her mind occupied.

Tomorrow, she'll be back at the Allegheny County Courthouse. Roy has appealed the judge's decision and has a new day in court.

Since last month's ruling in the Court of Common Pleas, Roy has done virtually no work on the house.

He hasn't fixed the roof.

He hasn't cleaned up the trash out front.

He hasn't even been around.

Until tonight, that is. He pulled up in his truck around dusk, and she spied him through the crack in her blinds as he unloaded tools and adjustable work lights just as the rain began to fall. The bandage on his head was nowhere in sight. She saw him unspool the extension cord and, as always, stroll down the street to his other house. He walked without crutches, and with no sign of a limp.

Soon after, she heard him making a terrible clamor.

From the sound of it, he's been down in the basement slamming walls with a sledgehammer. It's as if he's aware tomorrow is not going to go well—he's going to lose another battle—and all he can do is make noise in some kind of petulant, juvenile display of dissatisfaction. Either that, or he plans to bring the whole damn building down on himself.

Ann wants to ignore him, which is why she's turned to her piano.

If he is going to make a racket, she is going to make music.

As she glides her fingers over the keys, she hears the phone ring.

"Hello," she says, answering it as she peers out the window at the pouring rain.

"It's Marjorie. How are you holding up?"

"I'm fine," Ann says, and she means it. "Roy's making a terrible racket next door, but I'm ignoring him."

Despite the commotion, she is actually in high spirits. She feels there's no way Roy's appeal will hold up. He's done nothing to warrant a different ruling. And now that his bandages have disappeared, she knows for certain he was lying about that. Any sympathy she had for her neighbor is now gone. He's a liar. He's a charlatan. He's brought all of this on himself.

And even though he's no closer to fixing up his property, this has become a war of attrition, and Ann knows that eventually she'll win. He'll have to sell his house or have it repossessed. Someday she'll have a neighbor who will take care of the property. A neighbor she can feel comfortable living next door to.

And she'll feel proud that she didn't let Roy Kirk walk all over her.

She stood up for herself.

It's just a matter of time before Roy Kirk is out of her life altogether.

She doesn't say all this to Marjorie, just that she's confident and relaxed.

As they talk, Ann notices that the noise coming from next door has ceased. She checks the window and sees that Roy's truck is still outside. Maybe he's worked himself to the point of exhaustion.

Marjorie confirms that she and Ted will come by in the morning to pick Ann up for court. They'll all ride to the courthouse together.

"Sounds good," Ann says before hanging up. "See you bright and early."

She considers going back to her piano, but she wants to get a good night's sleep before tomorrow morning's hearing. She climbs the stairs to the top floor and puts the pan beneath the leaking ceiling, as she now does every time it rains.

As she's changing into her pajamas, she hears a loud crack of thunder, followed by a new noise. Like a stack of bricks falling over.

It's strange how sound carries in these row houses— this time Roy's racket sounded like it was coming from her own basement.

She listens carefully but hears only the steady drone of the rain against her roof.

She tells herself that she's spooking herself unnecessarily. In the bathroom, she washes her face and brushes her teeth.

She freezes.

Did she hear the creak of a wooden step coming from the stairwell?

You're just being paranoid, she tells herself, rinsing off her toothbrush and dropping it into the coffee cup she uses to house it.

As she steps over the threshold back into her bedroom, she catches a sudden movement out of the corner of her eye. Before she can turn her head, pain explodes through her skull.

Her world turns black.

When she comes to, she blinks her eyes, trying to

figure out what happened, where she is. She feels her body sliding across her bedroom floor. A hand is gripped firmly around her ankle.

Someone is dragging her through her own home.

CHAPTER 24

MARJORIE WILSON KNOCKS ON Ann Hoover's front door. There's no answer, and no sound coming from inside. She turns around and looks at Ted Fontana, who is sitting in the idling car, exhaust visible in the cool morning air. She throws her arms up to indicate her confusion.

He shuts off the car and jogs up the walk, still wet from last night's rain.

"She's not here?" he asks.

"No," Marjorie says. "And I talked to her last night. She knew we were coming to pick her up."

Ted knocks on the door, much harder than Marjorie did.

Still, there's no answer.

"Maybe she went to the courthouse on her own," Ted says.

"Wouldn't she have called me?" Marjorie says. "Or left a note?"

"You're sure she was going to ride with us? There was no miscommunication?"

"No," Marjorie says firmly.

They stand in the cold morning air for a moment, thinking. The extension cord that Roy uses for electricity is running up the sidewalk and into his front door, which stands about two inches ajar.

"Should we see if Roy is home?" Ted asks. "Maybe he knows something."

Marjorie gives Ted an incredulous look. "Are you serious?"

They've both been on Ann's side of the conflict from the start, so Roy Kirk no doubt holds a grudge against them. But Ted doesn't believe Roy would lie to them or treat them disrespectfully.

"Maybe something happened," Ted says. "He might know."

"He might have caused it," Marjorie says, keeping her voice low.

"You don't think...?" Ted says, trailing off, not wanting to say the words out loud.

"He scares me," Marjorie says.

They talk for another minute and agree that Marjorie should go wait in the car. Ted will knock on Roy's door. If there's no answer, they'll head to the courthouse and see if Ann is there.

"Maybe she just forgot we were coming," Ted says.

Marjorie is sure there was no miscommunication

between her and Ann, but she walks down the sidewalk to wait. She doesn't want to be close to Roy.

When Marjorie is in the car, Ted strolls to Roy's side of the row house. He raps on the door.

"Roy," he says, "you in there, buddy?"

Marjorie watches from the car, her nerves on high alert. She half expects Roy to come bursting out, raving and angry. She doesn't know what to expect with that guy. *Ted's too trusting,* she thinks.

Thirty seconds pass, and Ted knocks again, louder this time, really pounding on the door.

Marjorie holds her breath.

Still no answer. Ted heads back down the walk toward the car.

Marjorie isn't sure if she's relieved Roy didn't answer— or scared.

CHAPTER 25

MARJORIE AND TED ARRIVE at the courtroom. It's even more crowded than it was for the last hearing, but there's no sign of Ann. Roy isn't there, either. Both the assistant city solicitor and the lawyer representing Roy turn around anxiously. It's obvious they haven't heard from their client or witness, either.

"All rise!" the bailiff declares. "Honorable Judge Stacy Moreno now presiding."

Marjorie and Ted rise along with everyone else. The judge, a woman with glasses and short silver-gray hair, walks to the bench.

"Thank you. Please be seated," Judge Moreno says.

The judge notices immediately that Roy Kirk is not present, and when she brings this up, the solicitor points out that his primary witness, Ann Hoover, is also absent. Marjorie knows she has to say something.

She stands up.

"Your Honor, if I may," Marjorie begins, trying to control the fear in her voice. "I live in the neighborhood. We went by Ann's home on the way to the courthouse this morning. We'd made arrangements to all come together."

Next to her, Ted nods his affirmation.

"There was no answer at her door," Marjorie says. "I'm worried about her. I think something might have happened."

Judge Moreno thanks her and asks her to be seated. Marjorie's heart pounds as the judge considers her statement, then turns to the bailiff and asks him to contact the Pittsburgh Police Department, and have an officer go to Ann and Roy's row house.

"Let's get to the bottom of this," she says.

After the judge leaves the courtroom, Marjorie says to Ted, "I want to go back to Ann's house. We need to be there when the police arrive."

CHAPTER 26

PITTSBURGH POLICE OFFICER Jeremy Benson and his partner, Derek Schmidt, pull up in their squad car in front of the row house on Lawn Street. Nothing seems especially awry, except that one half of the row house looks like a very nice place to live and the other half looks like a disaster, with a trash-filled front lawn.

The front door of the disaster side is ajar, and the officers see an extension cord leading out from it and down the street.

They climb the stairs to the porch and knock on the nicer side, which is the address they were given for Ann Hoover. Both wear handguns on their belts, along with police radios and handcuffs.

There's no answer at Ms. Hoover's residence. As the officers discuss what to do next, they notice a man and woman hurrying up the walk toward them.

"Excuse me," the woman says. "I'm Marjorie Wilson. I'm a friend of Ann's."

Marjorie quickly explains that she is the one who prompted Judge Moreno to ask the police to check on Ann. As quickly as possible, she fills them in on what has happened between Ann and her next-door neighbor, Roy Kirk—and why it's so out of character for Ann not to have appeared in court today.

"There's no way she would have missed it," Marjorie says. "Not unless something was really wrong."

"Do either of you have a key to her house?" Officer Benson asks. Given the information Marjorie has provided, he feels there's probable cause to search the place, but he'd rather not break the door down if he can help it. Unfortunately, neither Marjorie nor Ted has a key. They look around to see if one is hidden somewhere, under the welcome mat or a flowerpot, but they can't find anything."

"I'll check around back," Ted says, and Officer Schmidt agrees to go with him.

Around back, the door is also locked, but Ted notices a rock sitting in a small planter, and under the rock they find a spare key.

Schmidt takes the key and carries it back around front. Benson asks Marjorie and Ted to go stand by the sidewalk and wait, then he brushes the mud from the planter off the key and slides it easily into the keyhole. A moment later, the door swings open.

"Ms. Hoover?" Benson calls. "This is the Pittsburgh police. Are you in there?"

There is no answer.

Both officers draw their guns and walk into the house.

CHAPTER 27

THE FIRST THING THEY notice on the hallway table is a set of keys, a purse, a wallet, and a file folder. Benson takes a quick look inside the folder and sees what are obviously the files Ann meant to bring to court today—photographs, transcripts from the previous court hearing, what looks to be a log of interactions with her neighbor.

Officer Schmidt checks the wallet. Ann Hoover's driver's license and credit cards are inside, along with some loose cash.

Benson and Schmidt give each other a look. They don't need to speak. They know what the other is thinking. It's highly unlikely that she would leave without this stuff.

Especially the wallet.

Nothing seems out of place in the kitchen. There are no dirty dishes in the sink. No evidence Ann had breakfast. The coffeepot is cool.

The living room is empty. A Steinway piano sits in a patch of sunlight streaming in through the window.

Yet something feels wrong here. Both men sense it. The house is too quiet.

They ascend the stairs, guns drawn. When they arrive in Ann's bedroom, both men spot the blood, a small red smear on the hardwood floor next to the bathroom.

"I'm calling for backup," Officer Benson says, grabbing the radio on his belt.

CHAPTER 28

MARJORIE AND TED PACE on the sidewalk, unable to stand still. The coolness of the morning has burned off, and the air has started to warm up. Marjorie feels too hot and takes off her coat. Then she feels too chilled and puts it back on.

She's a bundle of nerves. Every cell in her body is telling her that something is wrong. Very wrong.

The police officers step out Ann's front door, and for a moment, Marjorie hopes to see Ann with them. To hear that her friend just overslept. That everything is okay.

But Ann's not there.

The men are alone.

Marjorie starts up the walk, and one of the officers holds up his hand.

"Please stay back by the curb," he says.

She can hear it in his tone—something is wrong.

"Is Ann inside?" Marjorie says, her voice choked with fear.

"We did not locate her," the cop says.

The other man is speaking into his police radio.

Ted calls out to the cops, "You should check Roy's house."

The officer who held his hand up says, "We're going to."

Another police vehicle quickly pulls up to the curb, its lights flashing, but its siren off. One of the new officers from inside the car heads to the porch to talk to the others. The other one heads to Marjorie and Ted and asks them to maintain their distance from the house.

"My God," Marjorie says. "What the hell is happening?"

CHAPTER 29

OFFICER BENSON KNOCKS ON the door to Roy Kirk's place, which swings the door open another few inches.

"Mr. Kirk!" he announces, squinting to look inside. "This is the Pittsburgh police! Are you in there?"

When there's no answer, Benson pushes the door gently, revealing a dark corridor. What he can see of the floor appears to be littered with construction debris— broken plaster, tufts of insulation, glass, nails.

Benson pulls out a flashlight and shines it down the hall.

There's no sign of life in this house, either.

"Mr. Kirk," Benson calls into the house. "We're entering your residence."

He walks first, light in one hand, gun in the other. Officer Schmidt follows closely behind.

They aren't even five feet into the house when,

seemingly out of nowhere, a man steps into the hallway, squinting at the light shining in his face. He has long hair and a shaggy beard, and he isn't wearing a shirt. He's as thin as a skeleton, his skin as pale as white paint.

"What's going on?" the man asks. "Who are you?"

"I'm Officer Benson with the Pittsburgh Police Department," he says. "I called out to you but you didn't answer. Are you Roy Kirk?"

"Yeah," the man says, scratching his head. He looks like he's just woken up. "What are you doing here?"

"We're checking on you," Benson says. "You weren't in court today."

"Oh," Roy says. "That was today? I completely forgot. I've been so focused on my work here that it slipped my mind."

Schmidt keeps his flashlight in Kirk's squinting face, while Benson runs his light over the man from head to toe. Kirk isn't wearing anything but baggy khaki trousers and a leather belt. The man's pants are filthy and seem to be splattered with mud.

Benson pauses the light on Roy's feet. They're muddy, too—only the mud looks reddish.

"Sir," Benson says, trying not to give anything away with his voice, "would you mind if I had a look around?"

"Of course not," Roy Kirk says. "I have nothing to hide."

"Would you please step outside for a minute?" Benson says.

Roy walks toward the front door, and both officers

follow him. Once on the porch, Benson asks Schmidt and the other officers to keep an eye on Roy while he goes back inside to look around.

Out in the sunlight, some of the mud on Roy's pants now looks maroon, matching whatever is staining his feet.

Before stepping back into the house, Benson glances toward the street and notices a third police vehicle pulling up. This one is a police van. Also, the man and woman on the sidewalk have been joined by other neighbors.

A crowd is growing in front of the row house.

CHAPTER 30

MARJORIE GASPS WHEN SHE sees Roy, unable to hide her shock at how much the young man has changed since she first met him ten months ago.

He looks pale and emaciated. His bare skin is streaked with mud, and his pants, the only clothes he's wearing, are filthy. He looks like someone who's been trapped somewhere for days or weeks—dirty, starving, weak, and blinking in the unfamiliar sunlight.

"Is that blood on his feet?" Ted asks.

Marjorie feels like she's going to throw up.

A neighbor from down the street asks Marjorie what's going on. Others from the neighborhood association who'd been at the courthouse have also arrived. More police are pulling up, asking the growing crowd to stand on the other side of the street.

"Can you tell us what's happening?" Marjorie says, nearly in tears.

"No ma'am," the nearest officer says. "We can't make any statement at this time."

As they relocate to the other side of the street, Marjorie takes Ted's hand and asks him to pray with her. It's the only thing she can think to do.

CHAPTER 31

OFFICER BENSON WALKS INTO Roy Kirk's residence with a flashlight in one hand and his pistol in the other.

The house looks like a bomb went off inside. The walls are missing Sheetrock. Clumps of waterlogged plaster hang down from the ceiling. The air stinks of mildew. Benson's boots crunch as they step on dirt and glass and whatever else is littering the floor.

He arrives at the staircase leading up to the second floor.

The extension cord coming in from the front door runs farther into the house and, as far as he can tell, goes downstairs. He hesitates.

Upstairs or downstairs?

Benson chooses to follow the electrical cord.

When he arrives at the top of the basement steps, he sees light coming from downstairs. He eases down the stairs, each step creaking under his weight. As he descends, the smell in the air changes. The dank smell of mildew remains, but there's another odor on top of it.

The stink of meat that's just beginning to go bad.

He arrives at the bottom. Bright construction lights fill part of the room with harsh yellow light, but the basement is large and cavernous, leaving several areas in darkness. Trash is everywhere—fast-food wrappers and soda cans, newspapers and magazines, black bags and broken boards, bricks and chunks of concrete.

Benson scans his flashlight quickly past a mannequin lying on a pile of garbage bags. The mannequin, partly hidden in shadows, wears a wig but is missing its arms and legs. Benson shines his flashlight deeper into the cavern of the basement onto a cluster of tools— a masonry hammer, a circular saw, a hacksaw, a pair of tin snips.

The red liquid staining the tools is unmistakable.

Benson jerks the flashlight back to the dummy he's just swept past. His breath catches in his throat as he realizes what he's seeing isn't a mannequin at all.

CHAPTER 32

WHAT'S TAKING SO LONG?" Marjorie Wilson says, staring across the street.

The police officer—was his name Benson?—went into the house several minutes ago. Roy is standing in the yard at the bottom of the porch with three other officers, shuffling his feet impatiently, like it's merely an inconvenience that a whole squad of police have taken over his lot and are keeping a crowd of onlookers at bay.

Marjorie has a sick feeling that the police officer is going to emerge from the house and say nothing looks amiss. That they'll then drive away as if nothing is wrong.

But that's not what happens.

Across the street, the officer bursts from the house in a sprint.

"Arrest him!" the officer shouts. "Cuff him!"

Roy Kirk tries to run, but one of the officers grabs his arm. He twists free, but the other officers spring into action. One grabs Roy's other arm, and another wraps his arms around Roy's torso.

Roy kicks and flails. He clenches his teeth and growls like a rabid dog.

Benson jumps off the porch and joins the fray. Soon the four of them have Roy pinned down on the ground, his hands cuffed behind his back. He fights against the cuffs for a few seconds, then gives up. His body loosens, resigned to its fate.

"Oh, no!" Roy wails, his voice a haunting cry that Marjorie and the others will remember for the rest of their lives. "Kill me! Please, kill me!"

The men lift Roy and carry him bodily toward the police van while another officer pulls open the back door.

"Kill me!" Roy moans again. "Kill me!"

Chills race over Marjorie's body, covering every inch of her skin.

When Roy is locked inside the van, he thrashes around for a long minute, shaking the whole vehicle. His cries of "Kill me! Kill me!" can be heard outside.

Then the van goes silent.

Marjorie's hands cover her face. Her breathing is shallow. Everyone in the crowd is aghast.

The police are in a fervor, talking on radios, securing police tape in front of the property.

Marjorie can't stand it anymore. She marches across the street with Ted Fontana.

"You have to tell us what is happening!" she demands.

Officer Benson approaches with his palms raised. Something in his face, in the pallor of his skin, takes the fire out of Marjorie.

"Ma'am," he says, "we found the body of a woman in Mr. Kirk's basement. We haven't confirmed if it is Ann Hoover, but we suspect that it is. I'm very sorry for your loss."

Marjorie turns away and buries her face in Ted's chest, sobbing.

CHAPTER 33

WHEN POLICE COMMANDER Ronald Freeman arrives, Officer Benson escorts him downstairs into Roy Kirk's basement and gives him the rundown.

"Lord have mercy," Freeman says, looking at the carnage.

Ann's body has been cut in half above the waist, and her arms have been severed at the shoulder. The missing limbs are nowhere in sight, presumably already in trash bags. All that remains of Ann Hoover is her torso with the head still attached.

Benson shines his flashlight deeper into the basement and shows his commander a spot on the far wall where bricks have been removed, exposing a dark tunnel just wide enough for a person to crawl through.

"We believe he dug a hole through the wall," Benson says, "then snuck into Miss Hoover's residence on the other side, knocked her out, and dragged her back over here to try to dispose of the body."

"In all my years of police work," says Freeman, who was a detective for two decades before becoming commander of investigations, "I've never seen anything like it."

The two walk back upstairs as the crime scene investigation team arrives.

"Where does this go?" Freeman asks, pointing to the extension cord that runs from the basement, out the door, and down the sidewalk.

"The suspect owns another house just down the street," Benson says. "He lives there. Neighbors have told us he hooks together a bunch of extension cords so that he can get electricity from there to here."

Freeman says to Benson that he's going to send a team of officers to search Roy's primary residence.

Next, he turns to the police van holding Roy Kirk.

"You two," he says, addressing the officers who arrived in the van, "take the suspect to the station and get him booked."

"Yes, sir."

Freeman slaps his hand on the side of the van, making a hollow metallic ring.

The suspect inside makes no sound in return.

CHAPTER 34

POLICE COMMANDER RON FREEMAN follows the extension cords down the street to Roy Kirk's residence, where a crew of officers is already putting up police tape.

"Have you been inside?" Freeman asks a lieutenant.

"Yes, sir, and I think you're going to want to see this."

Freeman stops as soon as he steps over the extension cord and sets foot inside the house. The smell is rank—the air stinks of roadkill.

The front hallway is lined with small animal cages. Inside some of them, mice and hamsters scurry around piles of feces, clawing and biting at the tiny bars. In others, however, the animals are clearly dead, their bodies rotting and festering with maggots.

Flies buzz in the air and crawl up and down the walls.

"It gets worse," the lieutenant tells him.

Freeman peeks into the living room, which is as messy

as Kirk's other house, only instead of construction debris, this one is filled with magazines, newspapers, and more caged animals, some living and some dead.

He catches a glimpse of pages torn from adult magazines—naked men and women in leather bondage.

Freeman and the lieutenant walk upstairs, where another officer is standing sentry outside a door.

"What the hell is in there?" Freeman asks.

The lieutenant nods to the officer to open the door. When he does, Freeman is prepared for another horrific scene. Instead, he sees an ordinary bathroom, with a toilet, a sink, and a claw-footed bathtub with a shower curtain drawn around it. Nothing looks unusual—in fact, the room is quite a bit cleaner than the rest of the house.

The officer steps forward, his moves careful and nervous, and slowly draws back the shower curtain.

Coiled in the bathtub is the biggest snake Commander Freeman has ever seen. At least eight feet long and as thick as a two-liter soda bottle, the python slithers slowly toward the edge of the tub and pokes its massive head over the rim.

"We think the suspect raised hamsters and mice to feed to his pet snake," the officer says. "But for some reason, he stopped feeding all the animals and they started starving to death."

"So this thing's probably pretty damn hungry," the lieutenant says, gesturing to the python, which stares at them with cold black eyes. "You don't think he was dismembering the victim to feed to this thing, do you?"

"I don't know," says Freeman, whose stomach is tied in knots. "Let's get the hell out of here."

Once out in the hallway, he instructs the lieutenant to call animal control for help, then takes a handkerchief from his pocket and wipes sweat beading on his brow.

"This case," he mutters. "I don't think it could get any more bizarre."

He regrets his words a second later when another officer comes running through the house, his boots loud against the hardwood floor.

"Sir," he says to the commander, "we just heard from dispatch. You need to call the station. Something's happened."

CHAPTER 35

AROUND THE SAME TIME the commander was entering Roy Kirk's residence and seeing the first of the dead animals, Officers Larry Piper and Ricky Muñoz were driving the police van through the streets of Pittsburgh with Roy Kirk handcuffed and locked in the back. There's no window for the officers to see into the back; the only windows are on the rear door of the van, and they are protected by thick metal mesh.

Despite Roy's earlier agitation, they haven't heard a sound from the back of the van since beginning their drive. The station is only twelve minutes from the house on Lawn Street where they picked up the murder suspect, and Piper and Muñoz spend the time discussing what they know about the case.

"I guess the guy just lost it," Piper comments. "All of this, over a housing dispute."

"Just when you think you've seen it all," Muñoz says.

As they pull to the outer door of the jail, another officer steps out to greet them.

"Is this the murderer?" he asks.

"Let's be careful," Piper says. "He went ballistic when they arrested him."

Cautiously, Piper swings the door open, and the three officers look inside.

For a moment, it appears that Roy Kirk is lying down, asleep. But his head is not flat against the metal floor. His face, now a pale blue color, is suspended ten or twelve inches off the floor, held there by a leather belt coiled around his neck.

Despite his hands being cuffed behind his back, Roy Kirk had somehow managed to take off his belt, feed it through a gap in the metal mesh, and make a noose to hang himself.

"Call the paramedics!" Piper shouts, climbing into the van to loosen the noose.

Yet even when Piper gets Roy's head free, he does not gasp for air. Color does not return to his face. Muñoz tries to take his pulse, but blood no longer pumps through Roy's arteries. His body temperature has already dropped, and his skin is cool to the touch.

His empty eyes stare vacantly, with no sign of life behind them.

CHAPTER 36

TWO MONTHS LATER, Police Commander Ron Freeman sits on the stand of the Allegheny County Courthouse, ready to testify during the coroner's inquest into the deaths of Ann Hoover and Roy Kirk.

If Roy had lived, Freeman would be testifying at his murder trial. Instead, the city is holding an inquest to clarify the facts of the two deaths and to ensure that there was no wrongdoing on the part of the police in his death.

Instead of a prosecutor and a defense lawyer, there is only the city solicitor asking all the questions.

The courtroom is filled. Rebecca Portman, Roy Kirk's former fiancée, sits alone in the front row. Behind her Ann Hoover's family—her parents, her brother, and her sister. Many neighbors who knew both Ann and Roy are present, including Marjorie Wilson and Ted Fontana, who first raised suspicions that something was wrong.

Freeman has sat in numerous courtrooms over the years, testifying in murder trials or inquests, but he's never seen a courtroom atmosphere quite like this. Often courtrooms feel divided in two—friends and family of the victim on one side, friends and family of the suspected murderer on the other. Tensions are always high between the two camps. They cast hateful glances at each other. Sometimes words are said.

But not today.

Everyone present is saddened by the senselessness that left two people dead.

Everyone here is a victim.

For the last hour, Freeman has been explaining what the police believe happened. Sometime the night before the scheduled court hearing, Roy Kirk dug a tunnel from his property to Ann Hoover's and snuck inside. He struck her in the head with a hammer and dragged her, unconscious or at least unable to move, back over to his property, where he strangled her with an electrical cord. Afterward, he began dismembering her body and placing the pieces in garbage bags.

"We believe that when the officers showed up that morning, they interrupted what Mr. Kirk was doing," Freeman says. "Given another day, or even a few more hours, he might have been able to discard the body and cover up the evidence that he broke into her home."

In the audience, Marjorie weeps. Even though she'd been the one to raise the alarm, Ann had already been long dead by that point.

"Commander," the city solicitor says to Freeman, "let's talk now about the death of Mr. Kirk. How did this happen?"

Freeman explains that during the investigation of Roy Kirk's suicide, an officer attempted to re-create his actions. The officer put on the same pants and belt that Roy Kirk had worn, and had his hands shackled behind him in the exact same way.

They discovered, Freeman explains, that even with his hands behind his back, the officer was able to slide the belt through the loops of the pants until he could get his hands on the prong that fastened it. Once the belt was unhooked, the officer was able to take it off. Then, standing upright, with his hands still cuffed behind him, the officer managed to loop one end of the belt through the metal mesh on the windows of the van door, and was able to squeeze his head through the loop at the other end and use it as a noose.

"Mr. Kirk must have leaned down, causing the loop to tighten, and asphyxiated himself," Freeman explains.

The solicitor follows the explanation with a series of questions about police procedure when locking a prisoner in a police van. Freeman insists that the officers followed protocol.

"The ride to the police station is only twelve minutes,"

the solicitor says. "Is that enough time for him to do this? While bouncing around in a moving vehicle?"

"We believe Roy Kirk was dead before the van even left for the station," Freeman says, explaining that Roy Kirk had been in the police van for about twenty minutes before it left the scene to be driven to the station—a not unusual amount of time, he clarified, since officers were busy securing the crime scene and dealing with other matters.

It was true that no one had checked on Kirk before they left, but nor was it protocol that they *should* have checked.

"It's easy to second-guess what we might have done differently, but our officers followed procedure," Freeman says. "To commit suicide in such a way takes an incredible act of dexterity and determination. The bottom line is that Roy Kirk wanted to die, and nothing was going to stop him."

CHAPTER 37

YOUR HONOR," THE CITY solicitor says, "for my next witness, I call to the stand Rebecca Portman, Roy Kirk's fiancée."

Rebecca Portman, a petite woman with a haunted, haggard expression on her face, walks to the stand and is sworn in by the bailiff.

"I didn't know Roy was engaged," Ted whispers, leaning in close to Marjorie.

"I think there's a lot we didn't know about Roy," she whispers back.

Rebecca looks out at the full courtroom, every eye on her. She wants to burst into tears. She can't believe she is here.

"Ms. Portman," the solicitor says, "how well did you know Roy Kirk?"

"I thought I knew him well," she says. "But it turns out I didn't know him at all."

The woman describes how she and Roy had been dating for almost two years. But after he bought the eight houses—and specifically the house on Lawn Street next to Ann Hoover—he'd become increasingly stressed-out.

"He was depressed," she says. "He wouldn't talk about it, but I could tell. He became very distant. A different man from the one I thought I knew."

Rebecca says he stopped letting her come over to his house. He claimed he was receiving crank phone calls at the residence, and that someone had thrown firebombs at the building. One day she showed up unexpectedly at his house and found him with his head and leg in bandages. He claimed to have been shot; he limped and seemed to be in tremendous pain.

"The medical examiner found no evidence of gunshot wounds," the solicitor notes.

"I'm the victim of his bizarre deceptions," Rebecca says, "just like everyone else."

She says that she knew about the fines for his derelict property and about his feud with Ann Hoover.

"I asked him to let me talk to her—Ann," she continues. "I thought I could help alleviate the tension there. Find some way to compromise. But he wouldn't let me see her. He said he had everything under control."

When Rebecca's testimony is finished, the judge excuses her, then calls for a recess so he can meet one-on-one with the medical examiner who inspected the bodies. Thirty minutes later, court is called back to order.

The judge takes a deep breath and says, "I think we know as much about the deaths of Ann Hoover and Roy Kirk as we're going to. There's no dispute that late the night of March twenty-fourth or early the morning of March twenty-fifth, Roy Kirk tunneled his way into the home of Ann Hoover, abducted her, and murdered her. A few hours later, Mr. Kirk committed suicide while in police custody.

"What we may never fully understand," the judge continues, "is what happened inside the mind of Roy Kirk. What made this likable, seemingly ordinary young man go to such horrifying measures? We know he was under a lot of pressure. We know he was in a feud with Ann Hoover. We know he faced significant financial penalties. But, as far as I can tell, his own actions got him into that mess. And his own lack of action kept him in the mess.

"By all accounts, Roy Kirk was a friendly, likable gentleman. But murdering your neighbor over a property dispute is not what a normal, emotionally stable person does. Tunneling into a house shows premeditation. This wasn't a momentary crime of passion—he planned it ahead of time. Did Roy Kirk have a psychological break from reality brought on by stress? Did he snap? Or was he always a psychopath, hiding his true self from everyone? We may never know who the real Roy Kirk was.

"I think that is what's most disturbing about this case," the judge continues. "It makes you wonder how well you can ever truly know someone."

EPILOGUE

June 1, 2002

MARJORIE WILSON AND TED FONTANA walk down the sidewalk. It's a warm morning, and they're on their way to the grand opening of a new neighborhood park. Marjorie carries a bouquet of flowers. The two longtime friends say very little—despite the pleasant occasion, their mood is somber.

In some ways, today is a day of celebration. In others, it's a day of sadness.

The new park they're headed to is going to be named after their friend, Ann Hoover. Today would also have been Ann's fiftieth birthday.

But their hearts are heavy, because of course Ann did not live to see either her birthday or the park dedicated in her honor.

When they arrive at the park, they join the large crowd already gathered, enjoying hamburgers and cake. Church leaders and local politicians are scheduled to speak, and the North Hills High School marching band is assembled and ready to play a tribute to Ann, an alumna of their school.

The five-acre park itself is beautiful, with a pathway made of paving bricks leading through well-groomed lawns to a wooden gazebo standing as the centerpiece. The property was donated by Ann's friend, Jennifer Cavanaugh, and the township pitched in fifteen thousand dollars for the work. Another fifty thousand came from state grants, and another thirty thousand from the sale of commemorative bricks that line the gazebo floor. Even with all that, volunteers put in nearly two thousand hours of work, planting flowers, installing benches, and pruning shrubbery.

Ann's death had brought out the best in the neighborhood, bringing the community together to support the park project. Even people who had never met Ann came out to volunteer, getting their hands dirty in the kind of community-building effort she would have loved.

The end result is even better than anyone could have foreseen. The park is the perfect community-center space that Ann always hoped would be possible for the neighborhood. There are already plans to use the park for a summer community picnic, ice cream socials, and an Easter egg hunt next spring.

Marjorie and Ted watch as various speakers stand before a podium and discuss the project.

Jennifer Cavanaugh stands up to talk about how when

she was a little girl, Ann used to babysit her, and that before she died, Ann gave piano lessons to her young daughter, just like she'd given Jennifer when she was a child.

"Ann wanted what was best for everyone," says Jennifer. "And she loved this community. We want this park to be more of a celebration of her life than a memorial of her death."

The park includes a commemorative stone marker— almost like a gravestone—that reads:

ANN ALISON HOOVER MEMORIAL PARK
DEDICATED 1 JUNE 2002

Marjorie lays the bouquet of flowers she brought on the gravel at the base of the marker.

Throughout the commemoration, no one mentions how Ann Hoover died. But Marjorie assumes everyone, like her, is thinking about it.

After the ceremony, she and Ted walk back home via Lawn Street. They stop in front of the row house that Ann and Roy once shared. After the murder, the city impounded Roy's half of the row house, fixed it up, and sold it to new owners at a bargain price. Ann's family sold her property to a young couple hoping to make a good life in the neighborhood.

Today, both sides match, with new paint, freshly cut lawns, not a brick or shingle out of place.

There are no boarded-up windows, no garbage out front.

No extension cord running out the door.

No rats.

"It looks the way Ann would have always wanted it," Ted observes.

"The whole neighborhood does," Marjorie says, wiping a tear from her eye. "She always said this community had the potential to be something special. It's such a shame she couldn't live to see it."

"Do you think the people who live here now know what happened?" Ted asks.

"Of course," Marjorie says. "Everyone knows—even if no one talks about it."

As the two move on down the street, Ted says, "I don't know how they sleep at night, living in those houses."

Marjorie nods. She has nightmares every night about what happened. But where it happened doesn't really matter.

"It could've happened anywhere," Marjorie tells Ted. "All I know is, I'll never sleep again."

MURDER IRL

JAMES PATTERSON
WITH MAX DiLALLO

PROLOGUE

January 31, 2012

AS HE PULLS INTO the driveway of the white-clapboard house in Mountain City, Tennessee, Roy Stephens hears a sharp metallic squeal.

He winces. Not at the sound itself. At the scolding he knows he's about to get from his wife, Linda, shaking her head in the passenger seat beside him.

"How long have I been sayin' you need to replace those brake pads, Roy? A month now? Two? I guess someone's been too busy."

Roy sucks his bottom lip. Chooses his words carefully.

"Honey, I *have* been busy. And you know it. Picked up a couple extra jobs at the shop last week. Means extra pay. Thought you said you were happy about that."

"What about the week before, when y'all went trout fishing? Or the week before that?"

Roy feels a flicker of anger welling up inside him. He

loves his wife. Dearly. But lately, it seems they can't go five minutes without sniping and snarling at each other.

That's the reason they're stopping by this secluded house in the first place.

It's owned by a family friend, known affectionately around town as "Paw Bill," who's been letting Roy sleep on his couch these past few weeks while he and Linda work through their problems. Roy is grateful for the accommodations, but aside from him and Paw Bill, three other people—Paw Bill's thirty-six-year-old son, Billy Payne Jr.; Billy's fiancée, Billie Jean Hayworth; and the couple's seven-month-old son, Tyler—are living under this roof as well, so the modest home can feel cramped.

Roy doesn't know how long he'll be crashing at Paw Bill's, but he's told the post office to forward his mail here until further notice. This morning, he's coming by to pick it up.

"I'll be back in five minutes," Roy huffs to Linda, cutting the engine. "Unless I manage to screw that up, too."

Roy ambles down the driveway, enjoying the cool January air and winter sun. As he gets closer to the single-story home, he realizes both Billy and Billie Jean's cars are parked out front. *Strange.* Paw Bill leaves for work before dawn, and his son and future daughter-in-law normally head out an hour or two later. Roy can't imagine what both of them are doing home at 10:00 a.m. on a Tuesday.

He walks around the side of the house to the backyard, glancing at the small Pentecostal church in the distance, separated from Paw Bill's property by a grassy field. He gives the rear sliding-glass door a knock, then opens it. It's unlocked, as usual. That's common practice here in Mountain City—which isn't a city at all, but a rural, tight-knit community of only around twenty-four hundred souls. Peaceful and picturesque, nestled in the rugged foothills of the Blue Ridge Mountains in the northeast corner of the state, it's a place where crime and outsiders are both equally rare.

"Billy? Billie Jean? Y'all home?"

Roy shuts the door behind him and waits for a response. Hearing none, he shrugs, and picks up a stack of envelopes sitting on a nearby side table. As he flips through his various bills and credit card offers, he realizes that he still hasn't heard a peep. Not a footstep. Not a rustle.

And something about that just doesn't sit right.

Roy calls out again, louder. "Billy? Billie Jean? Paw Bill? Anybody?"

With a growing sense of concern, Roy sets down his mail and steps farther into the house. He creeps down the central hallway that leads from the kitchen to Paw Bill's bedroom, then on to Billy and Billie Jean's bedroom and Tyler's nursery.

The door to Paw Bill's room is slightly ajar. Slowly, Roy pushes it open.

He peers inside, sees nothing, and keeps moving.

Roy notices Billy and Billie Jean's door is wide open.

He looks into the room.

And gasps in abject horror.

Billy is sprawled on the floor, stiff and still, naked except for his boxer shorts.

His left cheek has been obliterated by a bloody, gaping gunshot wound.

His Adam's apple has been slit open by a deep crimson gash.

"Billy!" Roy screams as he rushes to the man's side. He gives the body a vigorous shake. It feels heavy. Lifeless. Cold.

Thinking fast, Roy dashes back down the hallway and bursts through the sliding-glass door. He races around the house to his car, crying out, "Linda! Come quick!"

"Roy, what in the devil are you so—"

"It's Billy! He's been shot! Come on!"

Linda stammers, frozen in place by her husband's shocking words. Roy doesn't have time to wait. He flings open her car door and practically drags her into the house.

"Dear God!" Linda exclaims at the sight of Billy's body.

"You still know CPR, right?"

"I...I mean, I used to! It's been years since the last time I—"

"Just try! I'll call 911, they'll walk you through!"

Roy runs back to the kitchen and grabs the cordless phone. He dials, returns to the bedroom, and hands the receiver to his wife, who is kneeling beside Billy now, tilting back his bloody head, listening for his breathing, searching for his pulse.

"I need an ambulance, bad!" Linda whimpers into the phone.

Roy crouches down next to her to help—when he hears a squeal.

But this time, it isn't worn brake pads.

It's a baby.

Without a word, Roy rises and hurries down the rest of the hallway.

The crying is definitely coming from the nursery.

Roy doesn't want to, but he makes himself look inside.

What he sees is worse than he could have imagined:

Twenty-three-year-old Billie Jean is lying motionless on the carpet, with a massive, oozing gunshot wound to the head.

Baby Tyler is curled up in his mother's protective arms, wiggling and wailing, apparently startled awake by all the commotion. He's splattered with Billie Jean's blood— but incredibly, seems physically unhurt.

Roy cries out in agony at the horrific sight of the brutally murdered young mother still holding her living child.

It's a savage crime. One that only a monster could commit.

Who could possibly have done this?

PART 1

CHAPTER 1

Three years earlier

MR. FLUFFY TAIL, YOU silly rabbit. You know you don't go next to Minnie. You go here. Between Piglet and Freddie the Frog!"

Jenelle Potter finishes arranging her small army of stuffed animals, then steps back to admire her work. Satisfied, she climbs into her bed alongside them.

Jenelle possesses the high-pitched voice and innocent manner of a child, but she wears the frumpy sweaters and narrow-framed reading glasses of a middle-aged librarian. She also stands a stocky six feet tall.

And she's twenty-nine years old.

Jenelle places her laptop on her knees and fires it up. She double-clicks on her browser, which she's set to automatically open Facebook and log in to her account. This shortcut only shaves off a few seconds, but for someone who checks social media literally dozens of times a day, those seconds can start to add up.

Jenelle spends the next hour mindlessly clicking and scrolling, skimming and "liking." Photos, news articles, status updates, political debates. Graduation announcements, job announcements, wedding announcements, birth announcements. She hands out digital thumbs-ups like candy, and she is a master of the modern art of leaving quick, chipper comments. ("So cute!" "OMG, gorgeous!" "Mmm, delicious!") It's a big, busy world out there, and Jenelle thrives on staying in the loop.

Then she clicks on her own profile page.

It's a much quieter space, with a whole lot less activity. Jenelle mostly shares inspirational quotes, random musings about her day, and pictures of cuddly puppies—stock photos she finds online, mostly of bulldogs, her favorite breed. She has a decently long list of "friends," primarily people she knew in high school, a few she knows only via Facebook. But nothing she's ever posted has received more than a handful of likes.

And honestly? That stings.

In an attempt to punch up her profile a bit, Jenelle clicks EDIT in her ABOUT ME section. But then she pauses. Summing up oneself in just a few sentences isn't so easy. After thinking for a bit, she types, "I'm a very sweet, caring person. I love life and I love to make others laugh."

Jenelle is about to write more when there's a knock on her open bedroom door.

"Hi, honey. Whatcha doin'?"

Barbara Potter, Jenelle's mother, hovers in the doorway.

She's a matronly fifty-nine, with curly, shoulder-length blond hair.

"Oh, hey, Mom. Nothin' much. Just been catchin' up with my friends."

"Seems like you're in front of that computer screen every minute of the day. Y'all must have a lot to talk about."

Jenelle pouts and folds her arms.

"When your only friends are *in* the computer, that's the only way to talk to them."

Barbara steps into Jenelle's room. She pushes aside some stuffed animals and lowers herself onto the edge of her daughter's bed.

"My sweet girl. I know how hard this move has been on you. How tough it's been for you to adjust. To fit in."

Barbara is referring to the family's relocation to Mountain City from Philadelphia.

Five years ago.

"I guess so," Jenelle replies. "I'm glad we're closer to Grandma and all. And this place sure is pretty. But the thing is, if you ain't from here…people just kinda look at you funny."

Barbara rests a gentle hand on Jenelle's knee.

"There may be some truth to that. But if the only 'you' they ever get to see is the one on the internet, how can you say that for sure?"

"What's my other choice? You know Daddy don't let me go out."

"Well, I can't say I'm crazy about it, either. There's a lot of bad people out there, honey. People who might not like you or accept you for who you are. Even people who might want to do you and this family harm."

"But not *all* of 'em are bad," Jenelle counters. "Right?"

Barbara sighs.

"Maybe your daddy and me...maybe we do worry too much sometimes. We just want to keep you safe is all. You're the most precious thing we've got."

Jenelle silently absorbs her mother's words.

"Now go wash up. It's almost supper."

Barbara pats her daughter's knee, leaves.

Jenelle returns to Facebook. Satisfied with her edits to her profile, she decides to quickly scour the web for a new puppy picture to share. After a bit of searching, she finds and posts a great photo of a cute brown-and-white bulldog being reluctantly dragged along by a short, tight leash.

It's an image Jenelle can relate to.

CHAPTER 2

...WHICH WE ARE ABOUT to receive, from thy bounty, through Christ, Our Lord..."

Jenelle's parents join her in saying "Amen."

The three raise their bowed heads and tuck into their dinner.

"Pass me those spuds, would ya, Jen?" says Marvin "Buddy" Potter, Jenelle's gruff, mustachioed father. Jenelle needs both hands to lift the heavy bowl of garlic mashed potatoes, but Buddy easily grabs it with only one of his massive paws.

"These pork chops are great, Mom. How'd you make 'em?"

"You're sweet, honey. I used fresh thyme and rosemary, straight from your father's garden. So thank *you*, Buddy, for having such a green thumb."

Buddy grunts, dismissively. "Couldn't kill those herbs if I tried. My rosebushes, on the other hand...and have you seen how pathetic my azaleas look this year?"

Jenelle gives her father's arm an affectionate squeeze. She knows that, after God, his family, and his guns, the thing he loves most in his life is his garden.

Not that anyone would guess that by looking at him. Buddy is a decorated former Marine who served with distinction in Vietnam. He wears a camouflage baseball cap emblazoned with the branch's Eagle, Globe, and Anchor emblem, and carries a combat knife and two holstered pistols, at all times—including at the dinner table. According to family legend, he even used to help the CIA run covert operations to rescue POWs, but that's not a topic he likes to talk about.

"I think your flowers look beautiful, Daddy," Jenelle says.

Buddy immediately softens. "Thank you, dear. That's nice of you."

The Potter family eats in silence for a few moments, until Barbara says, "So I saw something fun today in the town calendar on Topix. That's a website, Buddy, where folks around here like to post local events and messages and—"

"I know what Topix is. Just 'cause I don't use the internet don't mean I don't know what's on it."

"Well, anyway, there's gonna be an all-day spring bluegrass festival this Saturday in Stout Park. Doesn't that sound neat?"

"Not to me," Buddy grumbles. "I don't care for bluegrass."

"I don't much, either. But I was thinking…maybe Jenelle wanted to go. By herself."

Jenelle lights up at the suggestion. Buddy furrows his brow.

"I think it could be a good way," Barbara continues, "for her to get out and have a little fun. Maybe meet some other young people from around town."

"That's a great idea!" Jenelle says. "Can I go, Daddy? Can I?"

"Sure," Buddy replies. "Why don't you run and join the circus while you're at it?"

"Now, Buddy…"

"No way. It's outta the question. Just think about it, Barbara. Our daughter, surrounded by all those strange people? Drinking and smoking and doing drugs and getting into who-knows-what-else kinda trouble?"

"Daddy, come on. I won't do any of that stuff, I swear. It's just a concert right here in town. I'll be home before dinnertime. Please?"

Buddy drops his fork onto his plate with a loud clank. He glares at his daughter as if he were sizing up a Viet Cong prison camp guard.

"What part of 'no' didn't you understand? Now that's the end of it."

Jenelle doesn't mention it again, and after helping her mother clear the dishes and do the washing up, she retreats upstairs to her bedroom.

She turns on her computer and opens her browser.

Quickly checking Facebook, she sees her bulldog picture has garnered a whopping four "likes" and zero comments.

Frustrated and disappointed, Jenelle navigates to Topix, the website her mother mentioned, and skims the Mountain City community-events calendar. She finds the announcement for the bluegrass festival and clicks the link, which takes her to a website with photos from last year's festival, showing exactly what she was hoping for—and precisely what her father was so afraid of: an all-ages group of concertgoers, picnicking on the grass, some of them sipping wine, listening to music, having a blast.

The images fill Jenelle with a combination of longing and rage, especially the ones that show men and women snuggling or holding hands.

She slams her laptop shut and buries her face in her mountain of stuffed animals.

CHAPTER 3

MAIN STREET IN MOUNTAIN City is little more than a bank, a library, a greasy spoon, a hardware store, a combination convenience store and gas station, plus an old family pharmacy that's been serving the community since the Nixon administration.

This is the building that Jenelle enters.

All by herself.

She makes her way down the center aisle, past the mouthwash and shampoo, past the Band-Aids and laxatives, until she reaches the pharmacist counter in back.

A kindly, portly older man in a white lab coat and wire-rimmed glasses asks how he can help. She's there to pick up some prescriptions, she tells him. A lot of them. Not only for herself—Jenelle takes multiple medications to control her type 1 diabetes, among other chronic conditions—but for both of her aging parents.

It takes the pharmacist a good few minutes to gather up

all of the Potter family's prescriptions and set the nearly dozen white paper bags along the counter. Jenelle pays for them, stuffs them into her knapsack, and heads out.

But she gets waylaid as she passes the cosmetics section.

Jenelle has never been much into makeup. Or fashion. Or manicures or skin treatments or hairstyling or any of that superficial stuff. It's not because she doesn't enjoy looking her best. Who doesn't? It's because, even when she puts in the effort, she's never very pleased with the results.

Still, Jenelle idly inspects some of the items on display. She opens a pot of indigo eye shadow. Uncaps some lash-lengthening black mascara. Twists a tube of reddish-pink lipstick.

"That coral goes great with your skin tone."

Jenelle startles, as if she'd just been caught shoplifting, and drops the lipstick to the floor like it's on fire.

She turns to see a pretty, youngish brunette standing beside her. The woman is wearing an oversized blue vest, a name tag that says TRACY pinned on one side, and a warm, friendly smile.

"Oh, sorry...I wasn't...I mean, I was just..."

"It's okay," Tracy says, bending down to pick up the lipstick tube that has since rolled in her direction. "I didn't mean to scare you or nothin'. I just thought that color would look nice on you." Tracy's smile gets even bigger.

"Really?"

"Were you lookin' for something in particular, or just browsing?"

"Neither, to tell you the truth. I'm only supposed to be picking up prescriptions. I'm not allowed to stay too long. Or buy anything else."

Tracy nods. "Gosh, I wish I had that kinda discipline. Me? I'm practically addicted to buying makeup I don't need. You should see my bathroom. It's so cluttered, sometimes I can't even find my toothbrush."

Tracy laughs—so Jenelle does, too.

"I'm Tracy, by the way," she says, extending her hand. Jenelle eyes her nails—painted canary yellow, bedazzled with shiny little baubles—as they shake.

"I'm Jenelle. It's nice to meet you."

"I think I've seen you in here before. You live in town?"

"A little bit outside it. We're up on Hospital Road."

"But you didn't *grow up* around here, did you?"

Suddenly self-conscious, Jenelle shakes her head.

"Aw, I didn't mean it like that," Tracy says. "There were, like, a hundred kids in my high school class. And you and me look about the same age. I didn't remember you, so for a second I thought I was losing it. What a relief!"

Tracy chuckles again, so Jenelle follows suit.

"Um, you probably have to get back to work," Jenelle says. "And I promised my mom and dad I wouldn't—"

"Sure. I don't mean to keep you. But hey, maybe we could hang out sometime?"

Flooded with excitement and surprise, Jenelle just stares blankly at Tracy—for what feels to her like hours. It's closer to a couple of seconds.

"Try to control your excitement now," Tracy jokes.

"No, sorry!" Jenelle finally blurts out. "I'd love to!"

Bobbing her head, Tracy takes out a small pad and pen from one of the pockets of her vest. She scribbles something down, rips off the page, thrusts it at Jenelle.

"Here's my cell. My shift ends at four, most days. Call me anytime after."

Jenelle takes the slip of paper and marvels at it, as if it were a winning lottery ticket.

"Cool. Thanks. I can't wait to—"

"*Jenelle.*"

Jenelle turns to see Buddy standing by the pharmacy entrance. His arms are crossed tightly in disapproval.

"We've been waitin' for ten whole minutes. Just what do you think you're doin'?"

"Nothing, Daddy," Jenelle mutters. "Coming."

She gives Tracy an apologetic shrug, then follows her father out of the store.

CHAPTER 4

LIKE A PUPPY WAITING excitedly for her owner to arrive, Jenelle Potter has been anxiously huddled in front of her living room window for the past half hour.

Her new friend Tracy Greenwell should be there any minute.

This is the first time the two women will be socializing together. They've made plans to spend the afternoon at a nearby mall, which is about a forty-minute drive over the North Carolina border. To say Jenelle has been a nervous wreck all morning would be an understatement. She could barely eat breakfast or fall asleep last night.

Soon Jenelle sees a beat-up white Camry turn off Hospital Road and pull into the driveway. Tracy, behind the wheel, toots the horn and waves. If Jenelle had a tail, it would be wagging like crazy right now. She bursts out of the front door to greet her.

"Hey, Tracy!" she calls. "Can ya gimme two secs to finish gettin' ready?"

"No sweat, girl! Do your thing!"

Jenelle hurries back into the house and ducks into her parents' empty bedroom. She gives herself a final look, head to toe, in their full-length mirror, something her own room doesn't have. She adjusts her glasses. Straightens the hem of her sweater.

Takes a deep breath.

Exiting the house, Jenelle sees Tracy standing beside Buddy's lush purple petunia bushes, chatting with her parents. As she approaches, Jenelle can make out the tail end of the conversation—or rather, the interrogation.

"You're tellin' me," says Buddy, subtly adjusting the pistol and knife strapped to his hip, "that you're takin' my little girl across state lines?"

Tracy, unfazed, answers with a grin, "I guess technically that's true, sir. But I also plan on bringin' her back."

"Ever been in trouble with the law?" Barbara asks. "Arrested? Anything like that?"

"A couple parking tickets over the years, but I've paid off that debt to society. Literally."

"What about a number we can reach you at?" says Buddy. "Jenelle don't have a cell phone."

"Really? That's crazy. I don't know anybody this day and age under fifty who can survive without one. Heck, my eight-year-old cousin just got his first—"

"You got a number or not?"

"Daddy, relax," says Jenelle, finally reaching the group. "I left a note on the kitchen counter. It's got Tracy's cell, the name and address of the mall we're going to, and when we'll be back: six o'clock."

"And my blood type's B positive," Tracy quips. "Anything else?"

Neither of Jenelle's parents smiles, let alone laughs. Instead, Buddy takes off his Marine baseball cap and blots his perspiring, receding hairline. He and Barbara share a look.

"All right," he says. "You have our blessing. Anything happens, you give us a call right away. And if y'all ain't back on time...let's just say, we're gonna have a big problem. Understand?"

"You got it, Mr. Potter."

"Good. Now be careful out there."

"Thanks, Daddy," Jenelle says. "We will. Bye!" She gives both her parents a quick kiss, then she and Tracy head to the car.

"You girls have fun!" Barbara calls as Tracy starts the engine and drives away.

"Yeesh!" Tracy exclaims once she's turned onto the main road and picked up speed. "I thought I was meeting your parents, not your parole officers!"

"Sorry about that." Jenelle looks away, embarrassed. "I told you, they always like to ask my friends a whole lotta questions before they let me hang out with them."

"'Let you?' Jenelle...you're almost thirty years old," Tracy says, delicately.

"I know. So?"

"Never mind. Excited to let loose and get wild?"

"Yeah! I've never been to the Boone Mall before. I looked online, and they've got a sandwich shop and an ice cream parlor and..."

Jenelle trails off. She notices that Tracy has turned north on Cold Springs Road, toward the Virginia state border, instead of south, toward North Carolina.

"Uh, Tracy? I think you're goin' the wrong way."

But Tracy just laughs.

"You're not serious, are you? You didn't really think we were going to a mall?"

Jenelle feels her cheeks start to burn. "We're not?"

"You ever been to J.T.'s? They got, like, a million different beers there. And great music. A bunch of people I know are gonna be there."

"But...I told my parents..."

"Look, if you don't wanna come, that's fine. I can turn around, drop you off."

Jenelle feels stuck at a momentous crossroads. She considers her options. How disappointed Tracy might be if she backed out now. How furious her parents *will* be if they ever find out she lied to them.

At last Jenelle swallows her fear and proclaims, "Okay, I'm in."

"Atta girl," says Tracy as she merges onto the highway.

CHAPTER 5

JENELLE HAS DRUNK BEER before, but only some basic American lagers that her father keeps stocked in the fridge. Standing in front of this vast array of strange, multicolored taps—all brands and types she's never heard of—she feels overwhelmed.

"Do you know what you're having?" asks Tracy, flagging down the bartender.

"Um, maybe. What's an . . . 'eye-pah'?"

Tracy looks at Jenelle for a moment, then bursts out laughing.

"Really? You've never had an IPA before? Try one, maybe you'll like it!"

After Tracy pays for their round, Jenelle follows her to a large window booth at the front of this noisy, bustling bar. A few other twenty- and thirtysomethings are already sitting there. They look up as the pair approaches.

"Hey, y'all!" Tracy calls out. "Everybody, this is Jenelle.

Jenelle, this is Maggie and Jim and Becky and Lance and Ryan."

Everyone offers friendly greetings as Jenelle and Tracy sit down.

"Hello," Jenelle mumbles, and gives the group an awkward mini wave.

"Is she a friend of yours from work?" asks one of the guys, whose name Jenelle has already forgotten.

"Nope, but would you believe that's where we met?" Tracy holds up her pint in Jenelle's direction. "And I'm real glad we did. Cheers."

Jenelle clinks glasses. She takes a sip of her beverage.

And nearly spits it out in disgust.

"Whoa, you okay?" asks Tracy.

Wiping her lips, stifling a cough, and desperately avoiding eye contact with everyone around her, Jenelle answers, "Uh-huh. Totally fine."

The group slips into casual conversation. About work, about sports, about their dating lives, about their plans for the summer ahead. Jenelle tries to interject now and then, but she can't seem to get a word in edgewise. She mostly just listens, while forcing herself to take tiny sips of her bitter, undrinkable beer. She's barely made a dent in it when the others order a second round, then a third.

Finally one of the other women asks her, "So, Jenelle, what do you do?"

Jenelle gulps. Feeling the sudden heat of the spotlight.

"Um...nothing."

The group seems to be waiting for her to say more. *But what?* Jenelle wonders.

"I mean, nothing *yet*. I, uh...I'm from Pennsylvania. I just moved here."

After an uncomfortable silence, everyone politely nods and returns to their previous conversation. Jenelle slinks down in her seat.

She checks the time. It's almost five o'clock. If she's going to make it home by six, she and Tracy will have to hit the road in the next fifteen minutes or so. But Tracy seems in no rush to leave. She's thoroughly enjoying herself, and just ordered another beer. Even if she did want to head out, is she in any state to drive?

Jenelle feels her pulse start to pick up. She's way out of her depth right now. Almost on the brink of a panic attack. What should she do? Tear her new friend—her only friend—away from a good time? Risk the wrath of her parents? Or call them to come pick her up, beg their forgiveness, and maybe risk less of it?

Jenelle decides that this last option is the least terrible. She gathers up her purse and starts to slowly slide out of the booth.

Then she hears something outside. A low rumbling, fast approaching.

Jenelle looks out the window and sees a jet-black Ford Mustang come to a screeching stop in front of the bar.

Out of the muscle car steps a tall, slender, rakishly

handsome man in his early thirties, with dusty-brown hair and lively blue-green eyes.

The sight of him quite literally takes Jenelle's breath away.

But it makes Tracy and the others just smirk.

"Hey, look, everybody," Tracy says, loud enough for the man to hear as he enters the bar. "Casanova decided to grace us all with his presence."

The man laughs and bounds over to their booth.

"Ah, you're just jealous. The only woman in Mountain City who'll never get a date with me."

Tracy playfully swats the man and mimes throwing up. The others all laugh.

" . . . five, six, seven, plus me," the man says, counting everyone around the table. "That makes eight shots of whiskey. Be right back."

As he heads to the bar, Jenelle whispers to Tracy, as nonchalantly as she can, "Who *is* that guy?"

"Ugh. My *brother*. Word to the wise, Jen? Whatever you do, don't you dare fall for his charms. Unless you're *looking* to get your heart shattered into a million pieces."

Moments later, the man returns with a tray of shot glasses sloshing with amber liquid. He passes them out. Nervously, Jenelle accepts one.

"Now let's get this party started!"

The man thrusts his glass into the air. Everyone at the booth does, too, then downs their shot in one gulp. Jenelle sneaks a sniff of the liquor first, nearly gags from the smell alone, but pinches her nose and forces it down anyway.

"Mind if I sit here?" the man asks her, gesturing to the few inches of bench beside her. Equal parts flustered and flattered, Jenelle scoots over to make room.

"Uh, sure. No problem."

"I'm Billy," he says. "Billy Payne."

But Jenelle only nods in response. Her face blooms as she feels Billy's thigh press up against hers.

It dawns on her that she hasn't yet responded. "I... I'm... hi," she stutters.

"Nice to meet you, '*Hi*.' I think I know a friend of yours: '*Low*.'"

Tracy and the others groan at Billy's awful joke. But Jenelle giggles for real.

And her six o'clock curfew completely disappears from her mind.

CHAPTER 6

THE DRIVE INTO CHEROKEE National Forest is a breathtaking one, especially during the summer. From the passenger seat of Tracy's car, Jenelle Potter is staring in awe at the rolling hills and lush green canopy of trees in all directions.

She feels a hand tap her shoulder. She turns around.

From the back seat, Billy flashes her a heart-melting smile.

"Ain't it beautiful?"

Jenelle nods, bashfully.

She knows he means the natural scenery all around them. But a tiny part of her, deep down inside, is hoping against hope he means *her*.

Jenelle, Tracy, Billy, and the others have all hung out together a few more times over the past few weeks. Gradually, Jenelle has managed to convince her parents to allow this, even though they're still uneasy about it and have kept her strict, early curfew. Jenelle still isn't very comfortable spending time with the group "IRL" ("in real life"), as the expression goes. But she's ecstatic to have so many new people to talk to on Facebook.

As soon as she made it home from her fateful encounter with Billy at the bar—thankfully, only about ten minutes past her curfew, since Tracy had an evening shift at the pharmacy to get back for—the first thing Jenelle did was friend him on Facebook, along with everyone else she'd just met.

Since then, to her delight, they've all been exchanging messages and "liking" each other's posts with regularity. And any time she gets a like or comment from Billy, even a simple "Cute!" on one of her bulldog pictures, Jenelle's heart skips a beat.

Jenelle has also combed through every single photograph Billy has ever uploaded to the platform. In most of them, he's fishing with friends, playing pool, or toasting with a beer. But in plenty of others, he's mugging for the camera with all sorts of attractive women. Jenelle hasn't forgotten Tracy's warning about her brother's allure.

Still, she can't help but wish she were in some of those pictures herself.

Tracy pulls into a parking spot not far from the trailhead. "Here we are. Everybody out!"

Jenelle, Billy, and Tracy exit the car. They've come to Cherokee National Forest this afternoon to go on a scenic three-mile hike. Waiting for them are a few friends Jenelle recognizes, as well as a slightly older man she doesn't, who looks to be in his mid- to late thirties.

"Hey, Jenelle! Come here a sec," calls Billy, beckoning her over to the man. "Want you to meet somebody. This is Jamie Curd. He's me and Tracy's cousin."

Jamie's got a scruffy salt-and-pepper beard and is wearing a ratty baseball cap and a wrinkled plaid shirt that doesn't quite cover his prominent potbelly.

Jenelle says flatly, "Hello."

Jamie, his eyes glued to the dirt, murmurs, "Um...hey."

After an awkward pause, Billy laughs and claps them both on the back.

"I *told* Tracy you two would hit it off!"

Everyone soon falls into line along the trail and the hike begins. Jenelle had been hoping to snag a spot near Billy, to give them a chance to really talk—maybe even flirt. As much as she loves interacting with him on Facebook, being in his physical presence makes her feel another level of warm and tingly.

Instead, Billy has ended up at the front of the pack. Jenelle is stuck near the rear. Next to Jamie.

Great.

After a painfully long, awkward silence between

them, Jamie finally says, "So, uh, Billy told me you don't really have a job. And you're, like, always on the computer?"

Jenelle bristles. She isn't quite sure how to respond to that. Should she be flattered that Billy was talking about her in the first place? Or insulted?

"I look after my parents," she answers sharply. "That's my job right now. And so what if I like to use my computer?"

"I don't mean it like a bad thing," Jamie replies. "I'm on mine a lot, too. I'm no expert or nothin', but I've been teachin' myself how to fix 'em and stuff."

"Is that what you do for *your* job?"

"Maybe someday. For now I'm workin' at Parkdale Mills. The textile plant just down the highway. Same as Billy."

"I know where Billy works."

"I'm sure you know a lotta stuff. You seem like a real smart girl."

Despite herself, Jenelle smiles. She's been called many things in her life, but she can't remember ever hearing that.

After a few more minutes of hiking, Jamie adds, softly, "And I hope you don't mind me sayin' so, but you're real pretty, too."

Now Jenelle blushes. She's *positive* no man has ever told her *that*.

She gives Jamie another look, quite literally. He might

not be as conventionally attractive as Billy, or have his cousin's magnetic personality. But maybe, Jenelle thinks, she wrote this guy off too quickly.

"I don't mind at all, Jamie. In fact, you ain't too bad yourself."

CHAPTER 7

IN AN INSTANT, THE computer's familiar wallpaper and icons up and vanish. In their place appears an endless stream of garbled white text, scrolling rapidly against a harsh blue background, while the hard drive clicks and whirs.

Jenelle is watching Jamie Curd work his techno-whiz magic on her parents' home computer. She's sitting beside him at the desk in the living room, resting her chin on her hands in wonder.

Her mother happened to mention at dinner a few weeks ago that their aging desktop seemed to be acting glitchier than usual and running more slowly. Which immediately gave Jenelle an idea. She suggested they call her "new friend Jamie," a self-taught computer expert, to come over and take a look.

Jenelle knows her parents would never in a million years allow her to go on a solo date with any man, let

alone one they'd never met. So this seemed like an inge-
nious way to kill two birds. Her folks could get to know
Jamie, and Jenelle would get to spend some semiprivate
time with him.

Jenelle doesn't consider Jamie her boyfriend. At least not
yet. But she's hoping things are headed in that direction.
Jamie doesn't have a Facebook account, so she doesn't
interact with him on social media. Since meeting each
other about two months ago, however, they've exchanged
plenty of chatty emails. They also talk on the phone from
time to time—but exclusively in hushed, thirty-second
chunks at odd hours, since Jenelle is paranoid about her
parents picking up the landline and catching them.

She and Jamie have also hung out in person on a
couple of occasions, but only in group hangouts with
Billy, Tracy, and their other mutual friends. Jenelle revels
in the attention Jamie gives her in person, and genuinely
enjoys his company. Yet any time dreamy Billy is there,
too, it's hard to fully focus on Jamie.

"Disk reformat should take about an hour or so," says
Jamie, swiveling in his chair to face Jenelle. "Then I gotta
reboot the operating system."

"Wow, you really know your stuff," says Jenelle.

"Ain't that hard, really. I just ran a diagnostic and
followed the instructions."

"Well, *I'm* impressed."

Jenelle slowly slides her hand across the desk until her
fingers just slightly touch Jamie's.

"Done yet?" bellows her father, who has silently appeared behind them.

Jamie pulls his hand away and shoots to his feet. Jenelle once mentioned to him that her father was a former Marine with ties to the CIA. It clearly made an impact.

"Not yet, Mr. Potter, sir. Almost, sir."

Buddy squints at Jamie. Then at Jenelle. She's holding her breath. Hoping her father doesn't suspect anything. *Praying* he didn't see them almost holding hands.

"I think that's enough work for today," says Buddy.

"But, Mr. Potter, I haven't finished reinstalling—"

"Computer ain't goin' nowhere. Come by again tomorrow. Wrap it up then."

"Yes, sir."

Buddy turns and marches out, leaving Jamie chastened, but Jenelle relieved.

"I guess, uh . . . I should get goin'. Wanna walk me out?"

The two exit the house together and head toward Jamie's car.

"Thanks again for stoppin' by, Jamie. It was good to see you."

"You, too, Jen," he says.

But before he gets in his vehicle, he stops. Glances hesitantly back at the house.

"So . . . I got ya somethin'. But ya gotta keep it a secret. Okay?"

Curious, Jenelle nods. Jamie digs into his grimy jeans pocket and removes a small black object about the size of a deck of cards, as well as a long black cord. He slips them both into Jenelle's hand.

"It's your own cell phone. Now we can talk and text all we want."

"Are you serious?!" she gasps. "Oh, Jamie, I love it, thank you!"

Jenelle is equal parts shocked and thrilled. She steals a quick look at the phone, then clutches it close, burying it under the folds of her sweater. After peering back at the house herself to make sure the coast is clear, she leans in and gives Jamie a quick peck on the cheek.

Back in her bedroom, making sure she's facing away from the open door, Jenelle stealthily and excitedly inspects her new toy. It's a simple, outdated flip phone, but she still marvels at its slim profile and sleek design. It's one of the best gifts she's ever received. She's touched by Jamie's thoughtfulness. She can't wait to use it.

But first, after hiding the phone under a heap of stuffed animals, Jenelle opens up her laptop and logs in to Facebook.

She navigates to Billy's page—stifling a twinge of guilt—curious if he's posted anything new, hopeful that he's commented on something of hers.

Jenelle likes Jamie a whole lot.

But she just can't deny it.

What she feels for Billy is stronger.

CHAPTER 8

JENELLE POTTER WENT twenty-nine years just fine without a cell phone.

But now that she has one, she simply can't imagine ever living without it. Even after a few months, its novelty hasn't worn off. Every time she feels it buzz, she still can't help but smile.

"Just got us a table, c u soon!" she texts to Tracy Greenwell. The two are meeting at the diner in town for a quick lunch.

A moment later comes Tracy's reply. "Thx! be there in five."

Jenelle has shared her "secret number" with a few other friends as well, but the person who uses it the most by far is Jamie Curd. The pair texts dozens of times a day, from morning till night. They speak on the phone, too, often for hours at a time. Their conversations are usually about the most trivial subjects. Like what they had for breakfast. Their favorite reality TV shows. The weather.

But it's not the topics they discuss that matter to Jenelle.

She's just thrilled to have someone like Jamie in her life she can talk to.

Jenelle has also been vigilant about keeping the phone and its charger well hidden from her parents. She only texts Jamie when she's by herself. She only calls him when her parents aren't home, or late at night when they're both asleep. So far, they still seem totally unaware of their daughter's romance.

It's this blend of the familiar and the forbidden that makes the whole thing extra exciting to Jenelle. One minute, she and Jamie are exchanging pleasantries. The next, she's sneaking around like a secret agent. It's the most fun she's ever had.

If only I could get that kind of attention from Billy Payne.

Jenelle has finally come to terms with the fact that Billy just isn't a committed-relationship kind of guy. He likes to go out and have fun and not be tied down. He never seems to date any one woman for very long, so although Jenelle still holds out hope, she can't be too upset that he isn't dating *her*. At least they still have their friendship, both in person and on social media.

Although lately, these past few weeks, Billy hasn't been hanging out with the group as often. He also hasn't been on Facebook as much. Jenelle has been racking her brain, trying to figure out why. Did something happen?

Did she do something to upset him? All she knows is, the less she interacts with Billy—in real life or online— the more unhappy she feels.

Buzz-buzz. Jenelle receives another text, this one from Jamie: "Hi love, going on my lunch break, how r u doing?"

Tracy, still wearing her blue pharmacy employee vest, walks in just as Jenelle is writing back. The women greet each other, then turn their focus to the menu.

They're about midway through their meal, Tracy picking at a salad, Jenelle chowing down on a cheeseburger and chili fries, when Jenelle broaches the topic weighing so heavily on her mind.

"So, uh . . . how's your brother?"

"Billy? He's fine. Hopefully stayin' out of trouble."

"That's good. 'Cause I haven't really seen him much lately."

Tracy shrugs. "He's a busy guy, I guess."

"With work? Jamie said he doesn't think Billy's picked up any extra shifts."

"I'd be careful askin' your boyfriend about other guys," Tracy teases.

Jenelle giggles. "Ewww, stop! Jamie's not my boy-friend." Tracy smiles and rolls her eyes. "But really. Why doesn't Billy hang out with us anymore?"

Tracy hesitates before she answers—and not just to finish chewing.

"Maybe you should ask *him.*"

"Maybe I will. Maybe I'll send him a message on

Facebook. But he probably won't even see it. He hasn't liked any of my status updates or pictures or posted anything of his own in almost eleven days."

Tracy lifts an eyebrow. "How often are you stalkin' my brother's Facebook page?"

"Stalking? We're friends!"

Tracy sighs. "Jenelle, look—since *we're* friends, I hope you don't take this the wrong way. My cousin Jamie really cares about you. You two have somethin' special. I'd hate to see you throw that away over a silly little crush on my brother."

Jenelle is taken aback, embarrassed. "Crush? What are you talkin' about?"

Tracy gives her a look. "Fine. I'll just say one other thing: Be careful about carin' too much about what happens online. The internet can be fun and all, but at the end of the day, it doesn't matter. It's all just pretend."

Jenelle, hurt, averts her eyes like a scolded bulldog puppy.

She answers softly, darkly, *"I know."*

CHAPTER 9

MEMORIAL DAY IS A somber occasion in the Potter home. Jenelle's father, Buddy, lost a lot of close friends in Vietnam. Which is why he always insists his family treat the holiday with the solemnity and respect he feels it deserves.

But this Memorial Day, Jenelle isn't at home.

She's at a boisterous, boozy barbecue in Stout Park, along with Jamie Curd, Tracy Greenwell, Billy Payne, and many others.

"Nice arm!" exclaims Jamie as Jenelle manages to toss a metal horseshoe around a wooden spike set far away in the grass.

"Jamie," she jokingly chides him, "we're playin' *against* each other. You're not supposed to be happy when I score a point."

He shrugs and smiles. "Seeing you happy *makes* me happy. Sue me."

The two finish their lawn game, and also their beers. While Jamie gathers up the horseshoes, Jenelle heads to the cooler to grab them another round. Thank goodness they're all classic American brews she knows and enjoys.

As Jenelle fishes around the icy water, she sees Tracy approaching.

"Hey, Jenelle! I guess that old saying is true—great minds drink alike."

The two share a laugh. With Tracy is a slim, strikingly pretty brunette in her early twenties whom Jenelle doesn't recognize.

"Jenelle, meet Billie Jean Hayworth. Billie Jean, meet Jenelle Potter."

"Oh! It's great to finally put a face to the name," Billie Jean says warmly, extending her hand. "I've heard a lot about you."

Jenelle hasn't heard a thing about Billie Jean. She forces a smile anyway.

"Nice to meet you, too. How do y'all know each other?"

Almost imperceptibly, Billie Jean hesitates—and flashes Tracy a quick look.

"Uh, I just started a new job. At Parkdale Mills."

"Oh. So you must know Billy, too?"

"Hey," Tracy chirps, "why don't you go find Jamie and let's all get some food!"

Jenelle does. Soon she and Jamie are milling around the picnic area, piling their paper plates with grilled hot dogs and tangy potato salad.

But Tracy, Billie Jean, and Billy are nowhere to be found.

"Weird," Jenelle says. "I thought they'd meet us here. Do you see 'em?"

"Is that them over there?" asks Jamie, pointing to a cluster of people across the way.

"I think so. Here, take my plate and find us some seats? I'll go get 'em."

Jenelle marches through the park toward her other friends. But as she gets closer, she sees something that makes her stomach drop.

Billy and Billie Jean are holding hands.

No. They can't be.

Jenelle must not be seeing straight.

She walks closer to the group.

And witnesses something even more disturbing.

Billy drapes his arm around Billie Jean and pulls her close.

Then he leans in and gives her a kiss.

Jenelle stops dead in her tracks. Fighting to control a tempest of fiery emotions, she spins on her heel and scurries back to the picnic area, trying and failing to hold back tears.

"I hate this stupid barbecue, I wanna leave!" she wails to Jamie.

"Whoa, Jen, what's wrong? What happened?"

"I don't wanna talk about it. I just wanna go. Right now!"

With confused but tender concern, Jamie rises and puts his arm around her.

"Whatever it is, you can tell me. I'll do anythin' in the world to make it better."

But Jenelle angrily shoves him away. "Don't touch me. Just take me home!"

They barely speak on the drive back to the Potter house. Jamie tries a few more times to find out what made his girlfriend go from smiling to crying in mere seconds. But the whole ride, Jenelle keeps her arms crossed—and her mouth shut.

"Thanks," she hisses as they pull into her driveway.

"Jenelle, wait, please tell me what—"

But she's already hopped out of the car and slammed the door.

She would slam her bedroom door, too—if her parents allowed it. Instead, Jenelle plops down in front of her laptop and angrily fires up Facebook.

Within seconds she's searched for and found Billie Jean's profile.

Jenelle can't see everything on Billie Jean's page, since the two aren't friends. But the posts and pictures she *can* see leave Jenelle sick with jealousy and rage.

Photos of skinny, beautiful Billie Jean hanging out with friends. Opening gifts on Christmas morning with her family. Lying on a beach in a skimpy pink bikini.

Hugging and kissing Billy.

Jenelle starts to well up again. Her mind races. *How long have they been together?! How serious are they?! What could Billy possibly see in this stupid bitch?!*

Jenelle is about to slam her laptop shut—when she stops herself.

She takes a long, slow breath.

And clicks the tiny icon on Billie Jean's page labeled ADD FRIEND.

CHAPTER 10

BILLY PAYNE HAS BEEN *in lust* before, more times than he can count.

But in all his thirty-four, hard-partying years, he's never truly been *in love*.

Until now.

Since their chance encounter in the employee break room a few months ago, Billy and Billie Jean Hayworth have been virtually inseparable. Neither one was looking for a serious relationship—let alone a partner for life—but magically, that's what they found. Their chemistry together is incredible. Their connection, rich and meaningful.

Billy cares so deeply about Billie Jean that he's completely given up his formerly wolfish ways without so much as a second thought. He once loved cruising local bars and chasing a different woman every night. Now, he revels in quiet evenings on the couch with Billie Jean.

Talk of marriage and children used to send him running for the Blue Ridge Mountains. Now, Billy doesn't just enjoy having those discussions with Billie Jean. He actively looks forward to turning them into reality.

But one step at a time.

Tonight is the happy couple's first Saturday officially living under the same roof. Billie Jean has just moved into the white-clapboard home that Billy shares with his father. To celebrate, they've bought a case of beer, ordered a couple of pizzas, and invited over a few close friends, including Billy's sister, Tracy, and Billie Jean's childhood friend Lindsey Thomas, a peroxide blonde with a sassy disposition.

"To the incredible Billie Jean!" proclaims Tracy, hoisting her beer can high. "I don't want to jinx anything, but someday soon, I sure hope I get to call you my sister."

A collective *aww* fills the living room. Everyone clinks and drinks.

"You three, get together for a future family portrait," urges Lindsey. Billy, Billie Jean, and Tracy huddle close on the sofa as Lindsey readies her phone. "Say cheese, y'all!"

Once the photo is taken, Billy rattles his empty beer can. "Anyone else need another round?" He receives a resounding yes, so he heads to the kitchen to grab them.

Less than a minute later, he hears a chilling scream.

Billy rushes back into the living room to see Lindsey staring at the screen of her smartphone in total shock.

"Linds, what is it?" asks Billie Jean.

"I...I was about to upload that pic of y'all to Facebook...when I saw I had a couple mentions on Topix. You do, too, Billie Jean."

"So what? I post on that site all the time."

"You don't understand! I'm skimming through 'em and...they're horrible!"

Billy, Billie Jean, Tracy, and the others all huddle around Lindsey as she scrolls through and reads aloud a recent thread on the local community online message board.

"Somebody named Matt wrote: 'Billie Jean Hayworth and Lindsey Thomas are no-good whores who sell drugs and drink.'"

"Wait...what?" says Billie Jean, more incredulous than insulted. "Us?"

Lindsey continues, "Look at this one. A woman named Kelly posted: 'Yes, those two are whores. No-good people who have nothing else to do. They are nasty sluts. And don't Lindsey have HIV? That's what I heard.'"

"Oh, my God," says Tracy. "What a terrible thing to write!"

"And this one, too," Lindsey says. "From somebody named Dan: 'I know Billie Jean. That bitch has lived with more guys and had sex with 80% of Mountain City.'"

"It really says that?!" Billie Jean exclaims.

Lindsey shows her friend her phone. There it is, in digital black and white.

"Hang on a second," Billy interjects, still trying to wrap

his head around it. "Matt, Kelly, Dan...who are those folks? Do y'all even know them?"

"No!" insists Lindsey. "But that's the thing about Topix. Anybody can post anything under any fake name they want. Gossip, outright lies, you name it."

"But who would do that?" asks Billie Jean. "We haven't done nothin' to nobody!"

The group is stumped—until Tracy gets a creeping suspicion.

"Can I see your phone?" she asks Lindsey.

Tracy takes it and keeps scrolling. Then she shakes her head and sighs.

"So this guy named 'Dan'? He also posted, 'Jenelle Potter is a good girl and was brought up right.' Then 'Matt' responded, 'Jenelle is a sweet person and people try to get her. I love that she's not like Billie Jean and Lindsey. She stayed sweet. They are dumb assholes.' And then 'Kelly' said, 'Lindsey is so ugly, and she is mad because Jenelle is so pretty and sweet and nice.'"

"So it's *Jenelle* who's writin' all that crap about us?" asks Billie Jean.

Lindsey throws up her hands. "You think so, Sherlock?!"

"I always knew that girl was a little off," Billy says, "but this is goin' way too far!"

"What I wanna know is, *why?*" demands Lindsey. "And how come I'm gettin' *my* name dragged through the mud?! I've never even met this Jenelle, she just friended me on Facebook! I oughta punch her right in the mouth!"

As the group grows more and more agitated, Tracy steps in to try to calm everyone down.

"Okay, look...I probably know Jenelle better than anyone here. And I think I know what's happening. She's had a crush on Billy for months, and she's jealous of Billie Jean, so she's taking it out on her and Lindsey, by writing silly insults online."

Lindsey scoffs. "Silly insults? She's tellin' the whole town we're drug dealers, drunks, sluts, and whores! Hell, she's makin' up that I got HIV!"

"I know. It ain't fun to hear. But who cares? It's not like anybody reading Topix is actually gonna believe that junk. I think the best way to handle this whole thing is just ignore it. I bet Jenelle gets tired of her games and quits in no time."

Tracy makes a decent argument, but the others are skeptical. Especially Billy.

"I don't know," he says. "You really think this is gonna blow over?"

"What I think," Tracy answers, "is Jenelle is one sad, lonely, deluded person. But this is just some harmless internet trolling. What's the worst that could happen?"

PART 2

CHAPTER 11

WITH THE CUFF OF her woolen sweater, Jenelle Potter dabs her streaming tears and wipes her runny nose.

"They're so mean to me, Jamie! I hate them, I hate them, I hate them!"

Jenelle is curled up in bed, surrounded by her stuffed animals, cradling her secret cell phone to her ear. It's well past midnight and her parents are asleep, so she's trying to keep her voice low.

She's not doing a very good job.

"Jen, slow down. You ain't makin' no sense. You're sayin' they hacked you?"

"Yes, Jamie! How else would they get all those bad things about me on there?!" Jenelle is referring to a slew of cruel, insulting, anonymous comments that were posted on her Facebook wall earlier today.

"But how are you so certain it's them? And why would they do that?"

"I don't *know*, Jamie! But I'm *positive* they did it. Don't you believe me?" Jenelle has no way of proving that the anonymous posts were written by Billy Payne, Billie Jean Hayworth, and Lindsey Thomas, but she's absolutely sure of it. "I can't believe anybody would say those things about me. I deleted 'em all as fast as I could, but they really hurt. They called me ugly..."

"What? No way. They're just jealous of you, Jen. You're beautiful."

"They said I'm a loser..."

"That's crazy. You got a ton goin' for you."

"They said no one likes me..."

"Now I know for a fact that ain't true. I happen to like you a whole lot."

Jenelle cracks the tiniest smile. The cyberbullying from her crush and supposed friends seems terrible, but the support and comfort from Jamie feels pretty nice.

"Try to put it outta your mind, Jen," he says. "This is why I don't have Facebook or none of that stuff. It's nothin' but a huge waste of—"

Jenelle suddenly gasps and bolts up in bed.

"Shhh! Did you hear that?"

"Hear what?"

Jenelle listens closely.

"Some kind of rustling. It's coming from the backyard. Outside my window."

Jenelle stands and pads over to look outside. But it's too dark to see anything.

"Oh! And I just heard some kind of loud thud against the side of the house!"

"Are you sure? What kinda thud?"

"Jamie, hang on. I'm gonna go out there and check it out."

Keeping her cell phone to her ear, Jenelle slips on a pair of sneakers and starts to leave her bedroom.

"Jenelle, wait, are you crazy? Stay inside."

"I gotta know what's goin' on out there! What if it's Billy or Billie Jean? What if they came here to mess with me or somethin' in person?"

"Jenelle, it's almost o'clock one in the morning. It's not them, I promise."

Quietly tiptoeing down the steps, Jenelle answers, "You don't know that!"

Reaching the kitchen, she shuffles across to the side door.

"Jen, please don't go out there. Call the cops. At least wake up your father."

But Jenelle ignores Jamie's pleas. She unlocks the door, pushes it open, and steps outside into the backyard.

It's eerie. Nothing but darkness and crickets.

"Okay, so far, the coast looks clear."

Jenelle continues creeping along the grass, then stubs her toe against something heavy.

"What the ...?"

"Jenelle? Is everything okay?"

Using the light from her cell phone screen, she crouches down to have a look.

There, nestled in the grass, she sees a large, gray, oval-shaped rock, about the size of a brick.

"It's some kinda rock. I think they threw it at the house."

"They what? Who did?"

Jenelle looks closer. Something's written on it. Jenelle picks the rock up and inspects it. "Jamie...you ain't gonna believe this."

Written on it in Sharpie in big print letters is the name "Bill Payne."

Jenelle flips the rock over. On the other side is written "Billie Jean."

She turns it one last time. Written across the long side is, inexplicably, "I'm your huckleberry."

Jenelle instantly bursts into tears again.

"Billy and Billie Jean wrote their damn names on this rock they threw, Jamie!" she exclaims. "I told you they were after me! What if this is just the beginning? What if next, they want to hurt me, or worse?"

"Well...shit. Maybe this is more serious than I thought."

"What are we gonna do? You gotta send some kinda message back. You gotta make them stop!"

Jamie exhales. "Okay. Just stay calm, Jen. I promise I'll think of somethin'."

CHAPTER 12

A few weeks later

BILLY PAYNE SWALLOWS HARD, fighting the growing lump in his throat.

His now-fiancée, Billie Jean Hayworth, is lying in a hospital bed.

Her eyes are closed. Her body is still.

"You okay, baby?" he asks gently.

Billie Jean smiles nervously and answers, "Which baby are you talkin' to?"

They both laugh as she opens her eyes—and rests a hand on her growing belly.

Billy is still coming to grips with the idea of becoming a parent. Since finding out that Billie Jean was pregnant a few months ago, it's been a wonderful but wild ride. Along the way, he's experienced every emotion imaginable—but the one he's felt the most has been pure, unadulterated joy.

Soon the exam room door opens, and a woman in a white lab coat enters.

"Ms. Hayworth? Hi, I'm Nurse Chen. Are you ready for your ultrasound?"

Billy watches as the technician massages translucent gel on Billie Jean's stomach and begins the exam. Blurry black and white blobs dance on a nearby monitor. The technician fiddles with the controls. "Okay, give me one more second here..."

At last, the grainy image becomes unmistakably clear.

Billy is seeing his beautiful baby boy for the first time.

He feels an overwhelming, almost unbearable wave of emotion. He grasps his fiancée's hand in one of his, and with the other, he dabs away tears.

The technician gives both mother and child a perfect bill of health. The fetus's development and vital signs, she says, all look excellent. She instructs Billie Jean to continue looking after herself. That means taking her prenatal vitamins and trying to keep her stress levels to a minimum.

Which is a lot easier said than done.

Despite their hopes for a quick resolution, Billy and Billie Jean's problems with Jenelle Potter have only gotten worse over the past few months.

Both receive frequent Facebook messages from her calling them "mean," and demanding that they *"leave me alone!"* The couple has no idea what she's talking about. They haven't had any contact with Jenelle in weeks, online or off. As far as they know, none of their friends have, either.

The Facebook messages from Jenelle are annoying but harmless, and easy enough to delete and ignore. It's the truly vile insults posted on Topix that are the real problem. "Matt," "Kelly," and "Dan" have continued to spew hatred and spread false, disgusting rumors about Billie Jean and her friend Lindsey practically every day.

On the drive back with Billy from the health clinic, Billie Jean makes the mistake of checking the website on her phone.

"What the hell?!" she exclaims. "Oh, my God. Billy, you are never gonna believe what that bitch posted about us this time!"

"Billie Jean, come on. Put your phone away, baby. Don't even bother looking at that garbage."

"No! No way! Just listen to this! Just this morning 'Matt' said, 'Billie Jean is getting so fat with that baby. She looks like a chipmunk that's eating too many nuts, LOL.'"

Billy sighs. "Now if that's not the dumbest, most child-ish thing I ever—"

"'I hope she loses that baby. It don't need a mother like Billie Jean.'"

Now Billy starts to get angry. "You're lyin'. She really wrote that shit?!"

Billie Jean continues reading. "'And Billy, he's no father by the way he acts and talks.'" Billy seethes. "'I hope a bear would eat Billie Jean. Druggie whore-ass bitch. Go screw a damn tree for all I care. Leave Jenelle alone!'"

They're driving along a hilly country road—but Billy slams on his brakes.

"Damn it!" he shouts, pounding the steering wheel. "What is *with* that girl?!"

"I told you, she ain't right in the head!"

"Christ, you don't think I know that?!"

"Why are you yellin' at *me?*"

Billy reels in his rage. "I'm sorry, baby. I'm just real frustrated. I hate that some crazy chick we barely know is ruinin' what should be the happiest time of our lives."

Billie Jean reaches across the gearshift and takes her fiancé's hand.

"Me, too. So what are we gonna do?"

Billy looks over at Billie Jean. Then down at her stomach. He knows he has to come up with something—*anything,* and *fast*—to protect the people he loves.

"Least we can do is unfriend and block her on Facebook. We'll do that the second we get home."

"But what about all the stuff she writes on Topix? We can't block her there."

"There's gotta be some way to prove she's the one postin' all that shit."

"So what? Anybody can say anything on that site and pretend to be anybody!"

Billy's eyes narrow.

"Anybody can pretend to be anybody," he repeats.

An idea may be starting to take shape.

CHAPTER 13

BUDDY POTTER MAY BE the man of the house, not to mention the garden. But Barbara Potter is queen of the kitchen.

She's hardly a four-star chef, but she takes great pride in preparing simple, affordable, tasty meals for her husband and daughter. Tonight's dinner menu features herb-crusted catfish, scalloped potatoes, and a hearty spinach salad.

After chopping, peeling, and dicing for the better part of an hour, Barbara finally gets the fish ready for the broiler and the potatoes into the oven. With some time to kill, she decides to hang up her apron and check her email on the family desktop.

She clicks mindlessly through her inbox, skimming her usual batch of unimportant messages. Mostly newsletters, coupons, marketing blasts, junk mail.

But then Barbara sees an email with the most outrageous subject line: "Urgent!!! Top Secret—From The CIA!!!"

At first Barbara actually laughs out loud. She's received plenty of obvious spam in her day, but this one takes the cake. The actual CIA? Emailing her something "top secret?" Yeah, right. Why not throw in a Nigerian prince or two for good measure?

Barbara almost deletes it immediately, without even opening it.

But curiosity leads her to read it.

And she nearly falls out of her chair when she does.

It's a long message from a man who identifies himself merely by his first name, Chris. He says he was an old friend of her daughter Jenelle's back in Pennsylvania, and that he now works for the Central Intelligence Agency.

His job, Chris says, requires him to monitor on-line traffic all across the country. Recently, he's noticed Jenelle's name pop up in some suspicious intercepts from around Mountain City. To be more precise: in digital communication between a Billy Payne, Billie Jean Hayworth, Tracy Greenwell, and Lindsey Thomas.

Chris writes that he believes Billy is a secret member of a violent local drug gang, and worse—Chris has seen messages suggesting that Jenelle's life could soon be threatened.

Barbara covers her mouth in shock as she keeps reading.

Chris writes that he cares deeply about Jenelle, whom he remembers as a "good person." He doesn't trust the "dumb" local police to protect her, which is why he's getting personally involved by reaching out to Barbara directly.

Chris wants to keep the entire Potter family safe—and he'll do whatever it takes to do that. He has years of experience, he says, "getting rid of people in Russia and New York," and he's willing to use those skills again if that's what this mission requires.

The implication of his words is chillingly clear.

After telling Barbara that he'll be in touch soon with more details about the situation as he learns them, Chris ends his email by saying that he understands if Barbara has doubts about who he is and what he's telling her. To prove his identity, he's attaching a highly classified photograph of himself.

Sure enough, at the bottom of the email is a picture of a muscular white man in his thirties, with buzzed, dirty-blond hair, wearing a black collared shirt with a gold badge pinned to his chest. Barbara doesn't recognize him, but the photo does look authentic and convincing. She stares at it, long and hard.

Then she rereads the email—which is both the most absurd and most terrifying message she's ever received in her life.

Barbara is aware that her daughter has been bickering online recently with some of her former friends, and she has had the impression that the spat was escalating.

But had it really gotten so bad that someone might be plotting to *hurt* Jenelle?!

No. That's impossible. Ridiculous! The email from "Chris," Barbara thinks, must be a hoax. Some kind of a callous prank.

But what if . . . maybe . . . just maybe . . . it's real?

What if a kindly CIA agent really did discover that her daughter's life was in danger?!

Rereading the email a third time, then a fourth, Barbara feels herself breaking into a cold sweat. She debates what to do next.

Should she call the police, even though Chris specifically told her that they were incompetent?

Should she share the email with Buddy, who worked with the CIA himself years ago and might have some special insider knowledge?

Should she tell Jenelle, who has no way of knowing she's been playing with fire?

The loud beep of the oven timer jolts Barbara out of her indecision.

She fires off a rapid reply to Chris, deciding to treat him, his email, and his threat assessment against Jenelle as completely real. *Better safe than sorry.*

Barbara thanks the agent for getting in touch and bringing such a disturbing situation to her attention. She looks forward to hearing from him again. Until then, she won't breathe a word of anything he's told her to anyone—out of an abundance of concern for the safety of her loved ones.

Like Chris, Barbara writes, she's willing to do anything to keep her family safe.

Anything at all.

Anything.

CHAPTER 14

JENELLE POTTER FIRST VISITED scenic Cherokee National Forest almost two years ago. In the time since, her life has changed dramatically.

Back then, Billy Payne and Tracy Greenwell were among Jenelle's closest friends, and their cousin Jamie Curd was just a stranger.

Today, Jamie is Jenelle's devoted boyfriend, while Billy and Tracy—along with Billie Jean Hayworth and Lindsey Thomas—are her sworn bitter enemies.

Now that Billy and Billie Jean have their brand-new baby to focus on, Jenelle had hoped the group would dial back their cruelty. Instead, their constant online harassment and real-life intimidation seems to have only gotten worse. By Jenelle's count, they're posting more cruel things about her on social media from fake accounts than ever. She also believes they've been driving by her home late at night more often.

Jenelle's patience—and sanity—are wearing thin.

But at least for the next few hours, she vows to do her best to keep all of that out of her mind. She and Jamie are out for an afternoon hike, and all she wants is for them to have a pleasant, enjoyable afternoon together.

Except Jamie isn't making that easy. The hike was his idea in the first place, but ever since he picked her up, he's seemed more quiet than usual. Distracted, even.

"Think we'll see any deer out here?" Jenelle asks brightly.

"Huh? Oh. Maybe."

After traipsing along the trail for a while longer, Jenelle sees a large boulder up ahead. "Let's take a break and sit down for a minute," she suggests.

"Uh, sure. Okay."

And so they do. Passing her water bottle to him, Jenelle asks, "Jamie...is there somethin' on your mind? You've been actin' weird this whole time."

Jamie takes a long drink, then stares off into space, troubled.

"I ain't gonna lie to you, Jen. There is. It might sound crazy. It sure sounded that way to *me* the first time I heard it. But I got proof."

Jamie takes out a few sheets of paper from his jeans pocket and unfolds them.

"I've been gettin' these emails, Jen. From some guy named Chris. Says he's with the CIA. Really. And he says he's been watchin' that online fight you got goin' on with Billy and all of 'em."

Jenelle scrunches her face. "The CIA? Like, spies and secret agents and stuff? *They* know about Billy and Billie Jean hacking my Facebook and throwing rocks at my house?"

Jamie nods. "It gets worse. This Chris fellow says they got intel that Billy is in some kinda drug gang. Chris is workin' out a way to protect you... 'cause he says Billy and the others... they're fixin' to murder you and your parents."

Jenelle's jaw drops. She can only stammer, flabbergasted. "M-m-murder me?!"

Jamie bites his fist, emotional. "Is it true, Jen?"

"Is what true?"

Jamie shuffles the printed emails until he finds the one he wants. He reads aloud: "Chris also wrote, 'Jenelle really loves you, man. She has never loved anyone like she loves you. I see it all over her.'"

Shyly, Jenelle answers, "Yeah, that's true."

"I meant this next part. 'You have a great girl. I hope she don't think about killing herself. She has you to live for.'" Jamie looks at Jenelle, his eyes moist. "Is *that* true, Jen? Are you really so upset about all this that... you might actually...?"

Jenelle tries to stay strong, but she collapses into her boyfriend's arms.

"Oh, Jamie! I...I...I just feel so awful all the time! So angry. So helpless. They're all so mean to me and I don't know why! I'm ashamed to say it, but...

sometimes...ending my life is the only way I can think to make the pain stop."

Overcome, Jamie wraps Jenelle in his arms, squeezing her tight.

"Promise me you'll quit talkin' like that, Jenelle! And quit thinkin' it! All of this crap between you and Billy and Billie Jean...promise me you'll quit that, too!"

"But..."

"Whatever they're saying to you, I know it hurts. I know it's scary. I know it's gotten bad. Hell, the frickin' CIA is payin' attention! But you just gotta ignore 'em, Jen. Make 'em lose interest in you or somethin'. This ain't worth nobody dyin' over."

Jenelle sniffles. "I promise that...I'll try."

Jamie finally releases his hug. Then he reaches into his other jeans pocket and takes out a small black velvet box.

"I wanna make *you* a promise, too."

He opens the box. Inside is a simple gold band.

"Oh, my God! Jamie, are you askin' me to marry you?"

"Not yet. But someday. When we're ready. Until then, I want you to have this. To remind you how much I love you. I always will. I'd do anything for you."

Her hands are shaking, but Jenelle manages to take the ring and slip it on. She admires it as if it were a two-karat diamond.

"Thank you, Jamie. I love it. And I love you, too."

They embrace, then pull away.

"The CIA," Jenelle says, still in disbelief. "Think they're watchin' us right now?"

Before Jamie can respond, they hear a rustling in some nearby trees.

They jump. They turn. They look.

It's a mother doe and her fawn, slinking through the brush.

CHAPTER 15

BILLY PAYNE HAD NO misconceptions that fatherhood would be easy. He was ready for the sleepless nights, the constant crying, the stinky diapers. He was even prepared for the inevitable tension a new baby would bring to his relationship with Billie Jean.

What Billy *wasn't* counting on was still having to deal with drama from Jenelle Potter.

Despite all his efforts to make her stop, Jenelle has continued inundating them with paranoid, delusional Facebook messages and posting truly reprehensible Topix threads about them—lately, ones criticizing them for being bad parents.

Since Tyler was born a few months ago, they've both done their best to stay focused on taking care of their child and not obsess about every new, petty thing written about them on the internet, hurtful as it might be. Which is easy enough for Billy. He's still working full-time at the plant. Between his job and childcare duties, he barely has time to sleep, let alone scour social media.

But Billie Jean is on maternity leave. Though Billy has asked her—*begged* her—to cut back, virtually every time she puts Tyler down for a nap, she picks up her cell phone and goes online. Which invariably whips her up into a rage.

Tonight, however, Billie Jean is even more upset than usual. Billy has scarcely stepped through the front door when he hears sobbing—from both mother and child.

He hurries into the living room. Billie Jean is bottle-feeding Tyler with one hand, while furiously banging on her laptop keyboard with the other.

"Baby, what's wrong? What happened?"

"I can't take it anymore!" she exclaims. "Look! Just look what she wrote now!"

With dread, Billy moves next to Billie Jean and reads the screen.

Someone named "Mike" has written: "Billie Jean, why don't you shut your damn mouth, you bitch. One day, you are going to get beat up really good and left for dead. And your bastard baby. You won't leave here alive! I hope you die die die!"

Billy's eyes stay glued to the monitor. But he feels his hands balling into fists.

Insults, name-calling, slander—that's one thing.

But actual death threats?!

Jenelle has just crossed a bright red line. Something has to be done. Now.

"Baby," Billy says quietly, "take Tyler into the bedroom. I'll handle this."

Without questioning him, Billie Jean disappears into the bedroom with the baby. Billy grabs the cordless phone from the kitchen, looks up a number, and angrily dials.

After a few rings, an older man answers.

"Buddy Potter? Name's Billy Payne. I used to be friends with your daughter—until she started harassing the hell outta me and my family. We've tried to be patient with her. We know she has some issues. But now she's started sayin' stuff like she wishes my baby and my fiancée were dead! We're sick of it. We've had enough!"

"Now hold on there," Buddy sputters. "Whoever this is, you got some real nerve callin' me up and sayin' those things about my little—"

"Your daughter is making our lives hell! We don't want any trouble, but you've got to get her under control—or else!"

Buddy just grunts. Billy hears some rustling on the other end, followed by some garbled chatter. Then an older woman gets on the line.

"Hello? This is Jenelle's mother. What's this about her harassing someone?"

"Mrs. Potter, this is Billy Payne. I was tellin' your husband, I used to be friends with your daughter, until she started—"

"Did you say Billy Payne? Oh, yes. I know exactly who you are."

That's a bit of a strange answer. But Billy presses on.

"Like I was sayin', we don't want no trouble. We just want Jenelle to stop. Hell, I'd come up there and mow your damned yard for you if your daughter would stop calling me a bad father on the damned internet every three or four days!"

"Billy, I'm sorry...but I'm afraid I don't know what you're talkin' about. Jenelle is as sweet as can be. She's never done nothin' to nobody. I have it on good authority that *y'all* are the ones who have been harassing *her*. Making fake Facebook accounts, hacking into hers, posting all kinds of awful things about her. That's the truth."

Billy can't believe this. Jenelle's manipulation even extends to her own mother!

"Mrs. Potter, your daughter is lying to y'all!"

"I'm *not* lying! I only use Facebook to post dog pictures, that's it!" Billy hears Jenelle's girlish voice in the background. Has she been listening in? If that's the case, he'll address her directly.

"Jenelle, you know that ain't true! What about all the shit you write on Topix about us? What about—"

Jenelle suddenly breaks down into shrill, exaggerated wailing.

"Now look what you did to her!" exclaims Barbara. "I know you all want Jenelle dead. I know you all do!"

"What?" Billy is stunned by such a ridiculous accusation. "I do not!" he fires back. "I just want her to quit it! And maybe she'd know how to act like a normal person if you didn't keep her so sheltered in that house like a—"

"Leave us alone!" Barbara interrupts. "If you call here again, I'm gonna do something about it!"

"Not if I do something about it first!"

Click. The line goes dead.

Billy fumes. He had hoped the call to Jenelle's parents would make things better.

Instead, he has a terrible feeling he's just made his problems worse.

CHAPTER 16

BARBARA POTTER ONLY HAS one biological child. But over the past few months, she's come to think of CIA agent Chris as a surrogate son.

The two have started emailing frequently, exchanging all the latest details about Jenelle's situation. Barbara still thinks of Buddy and herself as Jenelle's primary protectors, but knowing she has a powerful outside ally keeping such close tabs on her precious daughter has been an enormous source of comfort and relief.

Especially after Billy Payne's hostile, threatening phone call. It really rattled her, but Chris helped Barbara keep the incident in perspective. The call, he explained, was just part of Billy's plan to frighten them and drive a wedge between her and Jenelle.

Luckily, his plan backfired. Barbara is now even more convinced of her daughter's absolute innocence—

and more concerned about her health and safety—than ever.

Which is why the CIA agent's latest email makes her literally scream with terror.

Sipping her coffee that December morning, Barbara sits down at the family computer and clicks on Chris's newest message. Subject line: "Urgent update!!!"

Chris tells Barbara that he's recently come across new digital intercepts suggesting Billy and Billie Jean are ramping up their harassment of Jenelle and setting their sights on harming Buddy and Barbara as well.

Even worse, he writes, he can now say definitively that Billy Payne not only "wants to hurt Jenelle," but that *"he is trying to take Jenelle's life."*

Barbara literally leaps up from her chair and shouts at the computer, "No, no, no! Y'all ain't gonna do that to my baby!"

After taking a few moments to compose herself, Barbara sits back down—and fires off an impassioned email in response.

"Billy and Billie Jean need to back off!" she frantically types. "We want peace, and no one here wants to kill anyone, but we will! We are ready to take care of this ourselves." Like a mother lion, Barbara concludes, "I'll do whatever it takes to save my young. I will kill if I have to. Not just hurt but kill!"

Barbara sends the email, then rises to her feet again.

Almost numb with outrage and fear, she starts to pace

around the living room, praying for some kind of divine guidance.

Moments later, her inbox dings. Chris has already emailed back.

He writes that he greatly admires Barbara's desire to protect her family at any cost. And apparently, she isn't the only one who feels that way.

Chris reveals to Barbara that he's also been emailing with Jamie Curd, who is "just as mad about how Billy and Billie Jean are treating you and Jenelle. He would kill too if he had someone to help him." Chris ends his email with "I think if he and Buddy would meet, it would be a good thing."

Barbara rereads that final sentence. Letting the suggestion sink in.

Buddy has met Jamie plenty of times before, but he doesn't know him particularly well. As Jamie and Jenelle's relationship has continued, however, Buddy seems to have warmed up to him, at least as much as her gruff husband can warm up to anybody.

When Buddy enters the living room from the kitchen, Barbara breathlessly decides to tell her husband everything. She prints out and shows him every email she and Chris have ever exchanged, well over a hundred pages. She shares every lurid detail about the violent threats the entire family is facing. She reveals Chris's latest suggestion that Buddy and Jamie get together.

Through it all, Buddy stays silent. Stoic. Inscrutable.

"Say somethin', Buddy!" Barbara pleads. "What do you think about all this?!"

Buddy's eyes grow cold and hard.

"What I think is...I better call Jamie."

As Buddy turns to leave, he and Barbara see Jenelle standing in the doorway.

Their daughter's horrified expression tells them she's overheard everything.

"Wait, Daddy," she whimpers. "You and Jamie...y'all ain't really gonna—"

"Of course not, honey!" insists Barbara, forcing a placating smile. "Nobody's gonna hurt nobody. Daddy just wants to talk to him, that's all."

Jenelle nods, but it's not clear if she's convinced.

"Jamie told me that CIA guy was emailing him," she offers. "I didn't know he was writing to you, too, Mom. And I had no idea"—Jenelle's bottom lip begins to quiver—"that Billy and them were planning to hurt y'all—or kill me."

"Now you stop that!" booms Buddy. "Nobody's layin' a finger on my little girl! Not if I have anything to do with it—and I sure as hell do!"

Tearfully, Jenelle heads back upstairs to her room. Buddy exits as well, vowing to reach out to Jamie very soon.

Once she's alone again, Barbara turns back to her computer. Still jittery and upset from the morning's events, she navigates to a Christian theology blog she often likes to read for comfort and inspiration. Barbara clicks around for a bit, skimming articles and comments, until she finds a piece that resonates with her to an almost eerie degree. Guiltily, she copies the link and emails it to herself immediately.

The headline reads, CAN GOD FORGIVE MURDER?

CHAPTER 17

January 30, 2012

THESE CHICKEN THIGHS ARE great, Mom. What recipe did you use?"

Jenelle Potter waits for a response. She knows how much effort her mother puts into making their family dinners, and how greatly she appreciates compliments.

But Barbara Potter says nothing. Her gaze is fixed downward. Her mind appears to be miles away. Jenelle turns to her father, but Buddy Potter looks similarly distracted. Neither of her parents seems to be eating much.

Jenelle clears her throat. Still no response. "Mom? Dad? Is everything okay?"

"Hmm?" Barbara says, suddenly snapping back to attention. "Just fine, honey. Have you tried the chicken yet? I used paprika. I hope you like it."

After dinner, Jenelle is washing dishes at the sink, up to her elbows in sudsy water, when she overhears her mother making a phone call in the living room.

"Hi there, it's Barb. I hate to call so late, but I got a credit card bill that needs payin' by midnight to avoid a fee, and this dang computer is acting up again, freezin' on me every five seconds. Would you mind... oh, thank you, Jamie, you're a godsend!"

Some thirty minutes later, Jamie Curd is in the living room, tinkering with the Potter family's desktop. Jenelle is sitting on the couch, happily watching him.

"What's that weird-sounding word," she asks, "that means the feeling you get like you've already done something before?"

Absorbed in troubleshooting the computer, Jamie shrugs. "Beats me, Jen."

"Well, that's what I got right now. Seein' you here, workin' away on the computer, makes me think of when we were first gettin' together. Remember, Jamie?"

Jenelle smiles, fondly recalling those early days in their relationship.

"I know bein' with me hasn't always been easy," she says, "thanks to Billy and Billie Jean. But you've always stuck by me. You've always had my back."

Finally Jamie stops typing and turns to her.

"Of course I have, Jen. I love you. You know I'd do anything for you."

Jenelle looks down at the gold "promise ring" she's wearing, the one Jamie gave her last summer, and smiles even bigger.

"I do know that. And I love you, too."

It's nearly midnight when Jamie finally finishes updating the Potters' computer. Standing by the front door, he hollers upstairs to Barbara that he's finished and heading home.

It's Buddy who comes down to say good-bye. Jenelle hovers nearby.

"Barb's going to bed but says thanks for the help. She appreciates it."

"Anytime, Mr. Potter. Good night, sir."

"Jamie . . . before you go . . . I'm askin' if you would also do *me* a favor."

Jamie looks confused. "Sure I would. What is it?"

"I've been doin' a lotta thinking. About all those emails you and my wife have been gettin'. Gonna need you to go for a ride with me. Ten minutes west on Highway 67, just past Swift Hollow Road. Think you can do that?"

Jenelle interjects, "Don't Billy and Billie Jean live around there?"

Jamie swallows. He looks at Jenelle, then back to Buddy.

Buddy scratches his beard. "Son, can you come with me or not?"

"Any time you need, sir."

Buddy claps Jamie on the shoulder, then heads back upstairs.

After Jenelle gives Jamie a goodnight peck on the cheek, she scurries upstairs as well and buries herself under her stuffed animals. She's feeling excited and scared at the same time and isn't entirely sure why. Why would her father be asking her boyfriend to come with him on such a short ride, and why would they be going to Billy and Billie Jean's part of town?

Retrieving her secret cell phone, Jenelle considers texting Jamie to talk about it. But she decides to hold off, and instead logs in to Facebook.

She's relieved to see her page hasn't been hacked since the last time she signed in earlier that night. Billy, Billie Jean, and their friend Lindsey Thomas haven't posted any new insults about her, either. At least not publicly. Jenelle is dying to check their personal pages, positive she'd find a trove of cruel words about her there, but all three of them blocked her months ago. *Jerks.*

Before Jenelle even realizes it, lost in her mindless scrolling and "liking," a few hours have gone by. Finally feeling sleepy, she logs off and gets ready for bed.

Dozing off, she hears her father's muffled voice coming from his bedroom. It sounds like he's on the phone. Who could he be calling at almost four in the morning?

Curious, Jenelle puts her ear up against their shared wall and listens.

"You remember that favor I asked you?" she hears him say. *"Can you do it this morning?"*

CHAPTER 18

OKAY."

That's all Jamie Curd says before hanging up with Buddy Potter.

Just one simple, single word.

But it may very well be the most consequential word he's ever uttered in his life.

Jamie shuffles into the drab kitchen of his ranch-style house and reaches for the fifth of Evan Williams whiskey sitting on top of his fridge. He unscrews the cap and takes a long pull. Jamie isn't much of a drinker, but if now isn't the right time to take a shot, when the hell is?

Jamie heads to his bedroom. He was awake when Buddy called him, fussing with his home computer in the den, wearing an undershirt and sweatpants. He changes into a pair of wrinkled jeans and a heavy flannel shirt.

As Jamie puts on his boots, hat, and jacket—and waits for Buddy—the full weight of what they might be about to do starts to hit him.

Jamie feels his knees start to buckle. He's standing stock-still, but he's out of breath. *I can't do this,* he thinks. *This is crazy!*

Buddy never made his intentions explicit. But he never *had* to. Jamie fumbles for his cell phone. He starts to dial the Potter house, intending to tell Buddy he's sorry but he's changed his mind, he's out, he wants no part in anything that's about to happen—when his phone chirps.

It's a new text. From Jenelle.

"He's leaving now. I hear the car. I love you, baby. I love you!"

The message hits Jamie like an emotional punch to the gut. He can practically hear the anxiety, the relief, the gratitude, and the affection in Jenelle's words.

All of which reminds him why he agreed to go with Buddy in the first place.

The woman he loves is in very real danger. This CIA-sanctioned operation is the only real way to ensure her safety.

To keep his precious Jenelle alive.

Tamping down his nerves, Jamie texts Jenelle back that he loves her, too. Then he puts away his phone.

Minutes later, a familiar black pickup truck pulls into his driveway.

"Morning, sir," Jamie says as he climbs into the passenger seat.

Gnawing on a toothpick, wearing a black leather jacket and his trusty camo baseball cap with the Marine insignia, Buddy simply gives him a curt nod.

The two sit in tense silence as they drive across town via Highway 67, a desolate, four-lane strip of cracked asphalt that cuts through the pitch-black Tennessee countryside. Finally, after ten excruciating minutes, Buddy turns right.

Into the parking lot of a Pentecostal church.

"What are you doing?" asks Jamie, suddenly thrown. Buddy never went over the exact details of his plan, but Jamie certainly wasn't expecting any part of it to involve a church.

Buddy doesn't answer. He finds a parking spot and kills the engine.

"Sir, the Payne house is a quarter of a mile away," Jamie continues. "Why are we—"

"Recon. From an elevated position."

Buddy takes a rifle scope from his pocket and holds it up to his eye.

"Target building is less than a fifth of a mile from our position, right on the other side of this sloping, wide-open field. Look for yourself."

Buddy hands Jamie the scope. He peers through it. Sure enough, there's a clear, direct line of sight to the home. He hands the scope back, feeling inadequate compared to a decorated combat veteran like Buddy, with his years of covert operation experience. "So now what?"

"We sit tight. And wait."

Calmed by Buddy's confidence but still a little uneasy, Jamie settles back into his seat.

CHAPTER 19

THEY DON'T HAVE to wait long.

"Look alive," says Buddy, squinting through his rifle scope. "We got activity."

At first, Jamie doesn't see anything. Then, off in the distance, he can just barely make out a car turn on its headlights and pull onto the road.

"Positive ident: Paw Bill," says Buddy. "Leaving for his shift, right on schedule."

Jamie is impressed—and spooked. "How did you know what time Billy's dad—?"

"No more chatter. Let's walk over."

Buddy starts to get out of the pickup. Jamie stays put, planning to slide over behind the wheel and wait for Buddy until he comes back to drive him home.

But Buddy glares at him. "Means you, too," he hisses.

"Me?" Jamie feels his fear bubbling up again. "But . . . you said I was just—"

"*Now*, Jamie. I'm giving you an order."

And just like that, Jamie's resistance crumbles faster than a sandcastle.

He and Buddy slowly make their way across the dark field toward the house. Jamie looks over at Buddy, but he can barely make out the man's shadowy figure. At this quiet hour, the dull crunch of dead grass under their feet is the only sound they can hear for miles. The only light guiding their way comes from the sliver of moon above.

Crossing the Payne property line, Buddy leads Jamie to behind a toolshed in the backyard. From the rear, the house looks dark and quiet.

But Jamie knows full well that two adults and a baby are fast asleep inside.

The whole thing is starting to seem like a bad idea again.

"Mr. Potter, what are we doin' here?!" Jamie whispers. "If Billy sees us, all hell's gonna break loose!"

"Shh!" Buddy admonishes. Then he crouches down, lifts up his left pant leg, and takes out a subcompact revolver from his ankle holster.

He holds it out to Jamie—who recoils in horror.

"No way, Mr. Potter! I can't kill nobody!"

Buddy snorts, irritated. "You ain't *got* to." He gestures to the sliding-glass back door. "I just need you to stand at that door and keep watch. Can you handle that?"

"But, why do I got a gun if I'm only—"

Buddy waves him off and skulks toward the house. Reluctantly, Jamie follows.

With the sleeve of his jacket covering his hand, Buddy gives the glass door a gentle tug. It's unlocked. Buddy softly opens it all the way. He points at Jamie, then at the ground, then at his own eyes, signaling *"Stay here and stay alert."*

Buddy steps inside the house, drawing a semiautomatic from his hip holster.

Jamie watches through the glass door as Buddy disappears down the hall. But the only thing he can hear is the thundering of his own heartbeat. He knows he's supposed to keep a lookout, but to calm his nerves, he briefly squeezes his eyes shut and tries to picture Jenelle. She's the whole reason he's here. She's what will help him get through this.

"What the hell?!"

Jamie hears Billy Payne's panicked cry from somewhere in the house.

He opens his eyes and looks inside. He hears more muted yelling, and glimpses Billie Jean dashing from one room into another. It looks like she's hunched over, as if carrying something in her arms. Baby Tyler? Or a weapon? Too dark to tell.

Blam!

A single, deafening gunshot rings out.

Jamie gasps and jumps back, as if struck by the bullet himself.

He stands there, stunned, frozen, for the longest forty-five seconds of his life.

Finally he sees Buddy reemerge and exit the sliding-glass door.

The former Marine levels a penetrating and inquiring look at Jamie—who knows exactly what Buddy is asking.

Jamie whispers, "Down the hall," and points in the direction Billie Jean ran.

Buddy spins and marches back into the house.

Seconds later, Jamie hears a woman's petrified screams—and a baby's piercing wails. Though muffled, there's visceral panic and terror in both.

Jamie shuts his eyes again, even tighter this time. He tucks the pistol in his belt and covers his ears as well. In his head, he silently begs Buddy, again and again, to show mercy to the mother and child.

Blam!

A second shot echoes from inside.

Billie Jean's shrieks abruptly cease.

And the cool January night settles back into eerie, absolute silence.

CHAPTER 20

January 31, 2012, five hours later

AS LINDA AND ROY Stephens pull into the driveway of the white-clapboard house, Linda hears a sharp metallic squeal.

Those darn brake pads! She's been asking him to replace them for months! Linda sighs. She really doesn't want to get into an argument with her husband this morning. They've been doing that plenty these past few months—so much so that Roy has actually been sleeping here at Paw Bill's house a few nights a week. He's even started forwarding his mail, which is what they're stopping by this morning to pick up.

Linda wants to be supportive, and hates to be a nag, but the two start bickering almost immediately when she brings up the brake pads. Before their quarrel can escalate, Roy gets out of the car and heads around to the back of the house.

Linda shakes her head. She wishes she and her husband

wouldn't fight so much. Then again, she reminds herself, at least she doesn't have the problems Billie Jean Hayworth has.

Billie Jean lives here, too, with Paw Bill's son, Billy, and their seven-month-old baby, Tyler. Linda has only met Billie Jean once or twice before, but she always found her a sweet young woman. So she was shocked a few months back when she was working at the gas station and noticed Billie Jean crying and screaming at two women in another car that was boxing her in.

Linda was in the middle of her shift, but she hurried outside to intervene. As she shouted to Billie Jean that she was going to call the police on her behalf, the second vehicle sped off.

Linda tried her best to help the hysterical woman calm down, especially after she noticed Billie Jean's newborn was in the car. Billie Jean told Linda the two women who drove off were Barbara Potter and her daughter, Jenelle, who'd been tormenting her for months—for absolutely no reason as far as Billie Jean knew.

"Tormenting you how, dear?" Linda asked.

"Threatening me!" Billie Jean answered, between sobs. "This won't stop! They called me trash. Said I shouldn't be here. And that I shouldn't be a mother! That I didn't deserve to have Tyler!"

Thinking about that day, Linda's heart breaks all over again. No stranger to difficult relationships herself, she hopes that whatever issues those women might have had, they're done and buried. Life is just too short to hold on to petty—

"Linda! Come quick!"

Linda turns in confusion to see her husband sprinting toward their car.

"Roy, what in the devil are you so—"

"It's Billy! He's been shot! Come on!"

Linda hears the words, but they're so shocking, she can't fully process them. So Roy yanks open the passenger-side door and starts all but dragging her to the house, down the hall, and into one of the bedrooms.

There, lying on the floor drenched in blood, practically naked, is Billy Payne.

"Dear God!" Linda exclaims.

"You still know CPR, right?"

"I . . . I mean, I used to! It's been years since the last time I—"

"Just try! I'll call 911, they'll walk you through!"

"Roy, no, wait!" she cries.

But her husband has already disappeared, leaving Linda alone with Billy's body.

Every instinct she has is telling her to look away— to *run* away—but Linda forces herself to try to help this poor man if she can. She creeps closer, kneeling down beside Billy's head. His left cheek is a gory mess, blown apart by what must be a gunshot.

It makes Linda want to vomit, but she fights that urge and begins to tilt Billy's head back to listen for his breathing. Doing so, she realizes his throat has been viciously slashed as well, exposing horrific bits of muscle and cartilage.

"Here, it's ringing!" says Roy, reappearing and thrusting a cordless phone at her.

"Johnson County 911," says the female operator.

"I need an ambulance, bad!" Linda blurts out.

"Okay, what's going on?"

As Linda starts to frantically explain, she notices Roy rush out of the bedroom again.

"Okay, is he breathing?" the operator asks calmly.

Linda leans closer and puts her ear near Billy's lips. Nothing. She presses her fingers around his spongy, gaping neck wound, desperate to feel a pulse.

"No! And I can't find . . . I can't find a pulse! All I see is blood!"

The operator says something in response, but all Linda can hear is a wailing baby.

She turns and sees Roy reenter the bedroom, carrying Tyler in his arms.

Linda screams, losing her last bit of control over her emotions.

"Oh, my God! Is he okay?!"

"Yes, yes!" Roy insists, tilting the infant forward so his wife can see that although Tyler is speckled with dried blood, he looks otherwise unharmed.

"What about Billie Jean?!" Linda cries. "Where's his mother?!"

Roy doesn't answer.

He doesn't need to.

Linda understands right away that this beautiful new baby has been orphaned.

She drops the phone and covers her face with her bloodstained hands, letting out a deep, primal moan.

PART 3

CHAPTER 21

TENNESSEE BUREAU OF INVESTIGATION special agents Scott Lott and Mike Hannon step out of their black Chevy Charger and into the midday January sun. They exchange not a word as they button their suit jackets and walk up the driveway to a modest white house on a sleepy gravel road.

It's been just over an hour since the two homicide victims were found. The crime scene, ringed with yellow tape, is buzzing with activity. Local police officers have secured the perimeter, taken statements, and begun canvassing for additional witnesses. Forensic techs, wearing full-body white suits, have started combing the property for evidence, inside and out.

Lott and Hannon flash their badges, duck under the yellow tape, and approach the open front door. But Lott stops before they enter, something dawning on him.

"Owner said he saw both victims alive before he left for work. Then he locked this door behind him. Always does. But he kept the back door open. That's how the first witness—the one who found the bodies—got inside, too. Right?"

Hannon shrugs. "So?"

"So, I wanna see *what* he saw, *how* he saw it."

"The witness?"

Lott gives his longtime partner a look. Hannon understands.

The killer.

The two men walk around the side of the home to the backyard. They note the large grassy field that leads to a tiny church. The toolshed. The sliding-glass door.

Lott and Hannon enter the house and move through the hallway to the body of the first victim. Male, Caucasian, age midthirties. Single gunshot wound to the head, deep laceration to the neck. The agents observe the partially clothed body and cluttered bedroom as techs take photographs and dust for prints.

"Perp hated him so much, he killed him twice," quips Hannon.

Lott nods. "A victim's throat is slit? That means it's personal."

They move on to the nursery, to the second victim. Female, Caucasian, age midtwenties. Single gunshot wound to the head.

Lott looks grim. "Witness says he found the victim's

seven-month-old son still in her arms. It takes a cold-blooded person to shoot someone holding a baby."

"Poor kid," Hannon says, shaking his head. He asks one of the techs, "Find any shell casings yet? Near either victim?"

"No, sir. We're still looking."

"Where are you with prints?"

"Nothing yet."

As Lott and Hannon exit the nursery and head back outside through the front door, Lott says, "We ain't gonna find shit."

"What makes you so sure?"

"This is one of the cleanest scenes we've ever seen, Mike. Two perfect head shots. No casings, no prints, no signs of forced entry, no eye-wits. And I saw a laptop, two smartphones, and a flat-screen TV in there, all untouched. This wasn't a B&E. This wasn't a sexual assault. This wasn't a crime of passion. This was a hit. Meticulously planned and executed by a highly trained killer."

Hannon runs a hand over his slicked-back, salt-and-pepper hair.

"Hoo, boy. That's quite a theory, partner."

"You got a better one?"

"We got two young parents, of modest means, no criminal records, living in the middle of nowhere, minding their own business. Who sends a hit man after *them*?"

Lott knows his partner has a point. But for now, it's the only hypothesis he's got. He turns back to face the house. Grasping for some kind of sense.

"I don't know *what* the hell we have. I just know that the son of a bitch is still out there. And we gotta catch him."

CHAPTER 22

February 1, 2012

WALKING UP TO THE front door of this quaint rural home, TBI special agent Mike Hannon says to his partner, Special Agent Scott Lott, "Ain't I always tellin' you to stop and smell the roses?"

Hannon gestures to the lush flower garden that takes up much of the front yard. Lott smiles flatly. He usually appreciates his partner's attempts at humor. But this morning, he's in no laughing mood. It's going on thirty hours since Billy Payne and Billie Jean Hayworth were murdered, and they're no closer to finding the killer.

After spending some time digging into the victims' lives, however, the agents did discover some kind of ongoing feud they seemed to be having with an estranged friend named Jenelle Potter. By all accounts, Jenelle is an odd one, sheltered and self-involved, with limited intellectual faculties. It seems highly unlikely that she could've had anything to do with Payne's and Hayworth's military-style executions, but with the investigation short on leads, Jenelle and her parents, Barbara and Marvin "Buddy" Potter, seem as good a place to start as any.

The agents are greeted at the door by a burly man in his sixties wearing a camouflage Marine Corps cap and a holstered sidearm and combat knife. They're accustomed to seeing folks open-carry weapons in public, especially in rural parts of the state. But it's not every day they see someone packing heat inside their own home.

"Marvin Potter? Special Agents Hannon and Lott, Tennessee Bureau of Investigation. We're hopin' to ask you, your wife, and daughter a couple questions about the murders of Billy Payne and Billie Jean Hayworth."

Buddy levels a suspicious look at the agents, but he betrays chillingly little emotion. "Heard about it on the news last night. Y'all think we're part of that?"

"We know Jenelle had some issues with the victims over the years," Hannon replies. "We're hoping to rule your family *out*."

Buddy mutters, "Everybody always points a finger at us for somethin'." But he moves aside and motions for the agents to enter.

Soon Lott and Hannon are seated in the living room across from Jenelle, Buddy, and Barbara.

"It's real sad. And scary," Barbara says of the crimes. "You just don't think something like that would happen here."

"How well did y'all know the victims?" asks Hannon.

"Not well at all," Barbara answers. "We'd see 'em in town sometimes. Say hello. But that's it."

"What about you, Jenelle?" asks Lott. He can't help but take note of this grown woman's awkward childlike demeanor, and her constant nervous fidgeting.

"Um, I used to be friends with Billy, I guess. But not anymore. Not for a while."

"As I understand it, you two weren't simply no longer friends," Lott presses. "Y'all had become more like enemies."

Jenelle looks at her parents, who nod reassuringly.

"That's because...one day, out of nowhere, they all just...turned against me."

"How do you mean?"

"Excuse my language, but they have been harassing the living crap out of me!"

Barbara puts her arm around her daughter to help keep her calm.

"Sayin' all kinds of awful things online about me," Jenelle continues. "Coming by the house sometimes, too. Late at night. Throwin' rocks and stuff. Tryin' to scare me."

"Why would they do all that?" Hannon asks.

Jenelle shrugs. "It came out to be a jealousy thing. They said I was too pretty."

Lott and Hannon share a subtle look. *Jealousy?* That seems...far-fetched.

Jenelle continues, "They said I wasn't from here, so

I was never gonna be accepted. I feel bad about the situation because I didn't want no harm on them. I *never* wished them harm."

"Of course you didn't, dear," Barbara says, patting her daughter's back.

Lott scratches his goatee. "Have you ever posted anything negative on the internet about *them?* Ever put on the internet that you wished they were dead?"

Jenelle vigorously shakes her head. "The only thing I had ever posted was 'Please leave me alone!' They were in my account. They hacked in."

Hannon is flipping through his notepad. He stops on a page and says, "Tell us about Jamie Curd. We understand he was caught up in this dispute as well?"

"He's Billy's cousin," Jenelle answers.

Lott adds, "He's also your boyfriend. Is that right?"

Buddy interjects, "Absolutely not. Jenelle doesn't date. Jamie's just a friend."

"A family friend," Barbara clarifies. "And not even a very close one."

Lott notices Jenelle open her mouth as if to say something, but she stays silent.

"But he's aware," Hannon says, "of the problems y'all had been having with the victims? That they were bullying Jenelle online, intimidating her here at home?"

Barbara replies, "I have no idea what Jamie did or didn't know about—"

"I was asking Jenelle, Mrs. Potter."

"Um...yeah. He knew a little bit. I told him some. We're...friends," Jenelle says.

"And whose side would he take?" Lott asks. "Theirs, I assume? They're family."

"No, he'd always take *mine*," Jenelle insists, "'cause I never did nothin' wrong!"

The agents start to wrap up their interview. Before they leave, Lott notices a wooden display case on the mantel containing various military medals and ribbons.

"Thank you all for your time," he says. "And Mr. Potter, thank you for your service. That's some impressive chest candy over there. You saw some real combat."

"I was just doin' my duty. Nothing more, nothing less."

"Guessin' you got to be a pretty good shot during the war?"

Buddy holds Lott's gaze for an uncomfortably long time.

"Average," he says.

Lott stares right back. And smirks.

"Why do I get the feeling you're bein' modest?"

CHAPTER 23

A few days later

MR. CURD? RIGHT this way."

Special Agents Scott Lott and Mike Hannon greet Jamie Curd in the lobby of the Johnson County Sheriff's Department headquarters, a low-slung building made of beige sandstone with gray and white trim.

Because the building doesn't have a dedicated interrogation room, the agents lead Jamie into the private office of the chief deputy, who's letting them use it for the duration of their investigation. Instead of a metal seat at an austere table under a bare lightbulb, Jamie—wearing a dark-blue jacket, a black baseball cap, dark sunglasses, and mud-speckled brown boots—eases into a plush leather armchair against the wall. Lott and Hannon take seats on either side.

Surrounding him.

"Thanks again for comin' down," Lott says, as easygoing as can be. "We really appreciate your help."

"You bet," answers Jamie, already looking uneasy in his seat.

"Before we get started," Hannon says, "we want to tell you three things. First, see that camera up there? This interview is being videotaped. Second, this is your one and only chance to be completely honest with us. Ain't gonna do yourself any favors if you lie. The truth *will* come out, and it'll only hurt you later. Even if you did nothing else wrong, lyin' to the police is still a crime. Do you understand, Mr. Curd?"

Jamie nods stiffly, then says, "What's the third thing?"

"Our condolences on your cousin's passing."

"Oh." Jamie looks down at the linoleum floor. "Uh, thanks."

"We understand you two were close?" Lott asks.

"Used to be. Not so much lately."

Hannon says, "Would that have anything to do with all the bad blood between your cousin Billy, his fiancée, and Jenelle Potter?"

"Uh…no. It don't. Billy told me that there'd been some emails or stuff posted. I don't have Facebook. I don't know nothin' about it."

"Did your *girlfriend* ever tell you what was goin' on?"

"Think she mighta mentioned it. Once or twice."

"So you knew there was some real tension there. Some real problems."

"Uh-huh."

Lott asks, "And you consider Jenelle to *be* your girl-friend, correct?"

Jamie nods.

"You love each other?"

"Yes, sir."

"Anything you wouldn't do for her if she asked?"

"No, sir."

"Let's say...some people were messin' with her. Harassing her. Real bad. Bullying her online. Saying terrible things. Even comin' by her house at night. What if you saw how upset it made her and she begged you to make it stop? What then?"

"Uh...I don't know."

Hannon presses him, "You don't know? Sure you do."

"I...I guess I'd call the—"

"Come on. You'd do what any real man would do. You'd take care of it yourself."

Jamie frowns. Squirms. Doesn't answer.

"Look here," Lott says. "It's our job to ask tough questions." He leans forward in his chair "Did you kill Billy or Billie Jean?"

"No," Jamie answers. Quickly and firmly.

"Did you participate or know they were gonna be killed before they were killed?"

"No," Jamie says again—this time, a tiny bit slower and less confidently.

"Who pulled the trigger?" Lott asks. "We're not looking to crucify anybody. We're looking for the truth."

"I don't know."

"Jamie, I think you do."

"I told you. I don't."

Hannon takes over, trying a different tack.

"Think about Tyler. Are you the type of man who would shoot a woman, probably begging for her life, with a baby in her arms?"

"No."

"No, you couldn't do that. But you know who did, don't you? Yes, you do."

"And before you answer," says Lott, leaning forward again and lowering his voice, ominously, "let me tell you this. Your eyes are a window to your soul. I can see your soul. And I've been looking right into your soul."

Jamie seems thrown by those words—but still maintains his innocence.

Lott sighs. He takes a moment to size Jamie up and regroup.

"Tell me about Buddy Potter."

Instantly, the fidgety Jamie freezes. Which tells Lott he's onto something.

"What do you wanna know?" Jamie finally asks.

"What's that relationship like? Him a military man, you datin' his only daughter."

Jamie starts to nervously twist his fingers together.

"It's...all right. We get along."

"Bet *he'd* do anything to protect her," Lott continues. "And I mean *anything*. All that training he got in the

Marine Corps? He ain't a man you want to mess with, if you know what I mean."

Jamie shifts again in his seat. Hannon seizes the moment.

"Did you and Buddy kill Billy and Billie Jean?"

Jamie's hand-rubbing has intensified. "No."

"But you know more than you're tellin' us. Time to come clean here."

After a few seconds, almost imperceptibly, Jamie nods.

"Who shot 'em?" Hannon asks. "Who had the gun?"

Jamie hunches forward in anguish.

"He did," he mumbles.

"He who? Buddy?"

Jamie draws a long, pained breath.

"Yes."

Lott and Hannon exchange proud, gratified looks.

They just cracked this case wide open.

CHAPTER 24

JAMIE CURD PICKS UP the receiver and slowly dials a number he knows by heart.

The phone feels oddly heavy in his hand, but at the same time, he feels a crushing weight has been lifted off his chest.

These past few days since the murders, he's been an absolute mess. While Buddy strolled out of the Payne house that morning as casually as if he'd been dropping off a casserole, Jamie had barely made it fifty paces back across the field before buckling over and throwing up. He's been trembling like a blade of bluegrass ever since. Unable to sleep. Unable to eat. Unable to get the sounds of those screams, and those gunshots, out of his head.

Of course, Jamie still believes their deaths were justified. Billy and Billie Jean weren't just making Jenelle Potter's existence miserable—according to a source deep inside the intelligence community, the two of them were actively plotting to kill her. Jamie might have played a part in ending two lives, but it was done to save another—the life of the woman he loves, no less. That's about as justified as any double homicide could ever be, even if the act itself is still agony to live with.

Which is why Jamie was so grateful when the detectives interviewing him showed him such mercy. After he shared with them the guilt and pain he was feeling as Buddy's accomplice, one of them said, "The truth shall set you free." Jamie had never really understood what that saying meant until then.

"Jamie? Is that you?" Barbara Potter says as she answers the phone.

He presses the heavy phone to his ear. "Yeah. Hi, Mrs. Potter."

"Chris just emailed, sayin' you were gettin' grilled by the police this morning. Is it over? How'd it go?"

"Fine. Better than fine."

"And they just let you go?"

"Yeah."

"Well, that's wonderful! We've been prayin' our hearts out."

"Thanks, Mrs. Potter. Um, is Mr. Potter there? Could I talk to him a sec?"

After some rustling on the line, Buddy Potter gets on. He's almost chillingly calm.

"Cops called ya down, did they? What for?"

"Well, they're, uh … pointing fingers."

"Pointing fingers?" Now Buddy's voice begins to rise. "They ain't got no reason to point no fingers at you or nothing!"

"Well, sure. I know that, sir. But I just, uh…wanted to call and, uh…you got rid of everything from Billy's, didn't you?"

There's a short but interminable pause before Buddy answers, "Uh-huh."

"Okay. That makes me feel better. Thanks, Mr. Potter."

The two men hang up. Jamie rubs his face, overcome with relief.

He eases back in his armchair, then turns to face Special Agents Scott Lott and Mike Hannon, sitting at a nearby desk, both wearing bulky earphones.

They've been listening in on—and recording—his call to the Potters the whole time. In fact, it was their suggestion that he make it.

"So, I did okay?" Jamie asks.

"You just got Buddy Potter on tape," Lott says, "confessing to being with you at the murder scene that night. Mr. Curd, you did a lot more than okay."

"And tell me again how doin' that is gonna help me?"

Hannon holds up his hands. "What happens next ain't up to us. It's the district attorney who'll decide what he wants to charge you with, and what kinda sentence to ask the judge for if you're found guilty. But I can tell you, DAs look a lot more favorably on defendants who help out and tell the truth than those who don't."

Jamie bobs his head. Understanding that jail time is almost certainly in his future, but satisfied he did the right thing—both several days ago and today.

Before the interrogation concludes, Jamie says, "I just got one more question y'all didn't answer that's been blowing about the wind."

"Shoot."

"Is the CIA here?"

Lott cocks his head. Hannon looks even more confused.

"CIA? No. Why did you ask about the CIA?"

"Because he, uh, says he works for 'em."

"*Who* works for 'em?"

"They call him Chris, but I don't know if that's his real name."

The agents glance at each other. "What in the hell are you talkin' about?" asks Lott.

Now Jamie grows concerned. He figured the Agency and the TBI would be working together on this, but maybe not. He wonders if he's said too much. If he's accidentally revealed something top secret. If it could get him into even more trouble.

"Uh, never mind," he says, trying to act indifferent. He holds out his wrists. "Now are you gonna arrest me or not?"

CHAPTER 25

February 7, 2012

SPECIAL AGENT SCOTT LOTT speaks into his dashboard-mounted walkie-talkie: "All units, target house is five minutes out. Be advised, suspect is ex-military, and known to openly carry at least one firearm. Proceed with extreme caution. No lights, no sirens on approach. Follow my lead. Over."

As Lott puts down his radio, his partner, Special Agent Mike Hannon, asks, "You really think sneakin' up on a guy who did multiple tours in 'Nam is a great idea?"

"Beats the alternative. We show up guns blazing, I guarantee he'll do the same."

"I meant, we could call ahead. No surprises. Let him know we're serving a warrant."

"So he can flush evidence and barricade himself inside? No thanks."

"Come on," Hannon scoffs. "We're dealing with a

law-and-order good ol' boy here. He respects the uniform. He'd never even think about—"

"Buddy Potter killed two innocent people in cold blood,
Mike. Including a mother who was holding her damn
baby. You really think a badge is gonna stop him?"

Hannon drops the argument and focuses on the country highway they're speeding along. Until something else
starts gnawing at him.

"One thing Curd said I just can't get outta my mind."

Lott snickers. "Lemme guess. When he asked us where
'Chris' from the Central freakin' Intelligence Agency
was?"

"Why would he say something like that out of the
blue? What's that even mean? It's the only part of his story
that really don't make any sense. And Barbara mentioned
Chris, too, when Curd called the Potters. Said she'd just
gotten an email from him."

"Partner, this is all one big, messed-up puzzle. We got
lots of pieces that don't make any sense yet. Let's deal
with one at a time."

Minutes later, with five other state and local police
vehicles in tow, Lott and Hannon's Charger rolls to a
stop in front of the Potter house. They and ten other law
enforcement officers exit and start to fan out around the
property.

Lott, Hannon, and a pair of officers head directly to
the front door. As they get near, Buddy throws it open,
steps out, and scowls at them.

As usual, he's wearing his camo Marine cap and a pistol in his hip holster.

"Now what on God's green earth is this about?"

"Marvin E. Potter Jr.," Lott reads with authority from a multipage document, "in accordance with title forty, section six, chapter two of the criminal code of the State of Tennessee, a warrant has been duly issued for your arrest in connection with the homicides of Billie Jean Hayworth and Billy Clay Payne."

"Now wait a minute. Y'all are arresting me?"

The agents and officers step closer to Buddy.

"Mr. Potter, please turn around and place your hands behind your back."

"I'll put my hands wherever I please. This is outrageous."

"Mr. Potter..."

"Y'all are just wasting time. Yours and mine."

"I'll remind you, you have the right to remain silent."

"Oh, I know my damn rights. I've spilled my own blood defendin' them!"

Lott, Hannon, and the officers now have Buddy surrounded—which only seems to put him more on edge.

"Mr. Potter, I'm going to ask you one more time. Turn around and place your—"

"He's goin' for his gun!" Hannon shouts.

Thinking fast, Hannon and Lott lunge at Buddy—and forcibly grab hold of the older man's arms.

His pistol never leaves its holster.

Neither does the concealed mini revolver in his ankle holster.

Nor does the combat knife on his belt leave its sheath.

All those weapons are seized and catalogued as Buddy is led into a cruiser, and Lott, Hannon, and the officers begin their search of the Potters' house and property.

CHAPTER 26

TENNESSEE BUREAU OF INVESTIGATION

Special Agents Scott Lott and Mike Hannon find nearly sixty firearms—handguns, shotguns, rifles, even an AK-47; enough weaponry to equip a small army—in the basement alone.

The search of the Potter family home is fastidious and lasts multiple hours, during which time Jenelle and Barbara Potter have been instructed to sit quietly on the living room sofa. They can only watch, visibly uneasy, as their house is turned upside down. They seem especially upset when officers cart away Jenelle's laptop and the family's desktop computer, both of which will be sent off to be examined by digital forensic technicians at the state crime lab.

Officers open every closet, cabinet, and drawer. They look under—and inside—every couch cushion, pillow, and mattress. They thumb through every page of every magazine and book. Hunting for secret cubbies and hidden crawl spaces, they inspect every wall, ceiling, and floorboard. As the search starts to wind down, however, little hard evidence has been found linking anyone in the family to the murders of Billy Payne and Billie Jean Hayworth.

But then Lott discovers something odd while sifting through stacks of papers on the desk in the living room. He comes upon a picture of Billie Jean that looks to have been printed off the internet. It's a candid shot of her at an outdoor café with a group of friends. *How strange,* Lott thinks. *This is the woman who was allegedly torturing Jenelle, day in and day out. Why would the Potters have a personal photograph of her?*

Lott continues looking and soon finds additional pictures of Billie Jean. In one, she's washing her car. In another, she and some friends are rock climbing. In a third, she's lying on a beach, wearing a pink bikini.

On the top of this last photo, the words *Billie Whore* have been written in black Sharpie.

Lott considers asking Jenelle and Barbara about the pictures, but he decides to keep quiet. He gathers them all up in a pile, intending to bag and catalogue them later, and sets them down on a chair near the couch where the women are sitting.

"What are those?" Barbara asks, craning her neck to get a look.

"Possible evidence, ma'am," Lott responds. "Need you to stay seated, please."

Lott goes back to searching the living room—when a moment later, out of the corner of his eye, he sees Barbara get up, grab the stack of photos, and start to tear them down the middle.

"Hey, stop that!" Lott calls out.

He rushes over and just barely manages to snatch the pages out of her hands before she does too much damage. Frankly, that Barbara brazenly attempted to destroy these photographs right in front of him tells Lott they may be even more important than he'd realized.

"Now sit back down!" he commands. "And don't either of y'all try that again unless you'd rather wait in the back of a squad car."

Once the search of the house is complete, Lott and Hannon shift their focus to Buddy's pickup truck. They inspect every inch of it, from top to bottom— here, too, looking for secret compartments and hiding spots.

But that isn't necessary. A great deal of evidence is sitting out in plain sight. In the center console is a handful of loose .38 bullets, the same caliber as the ones that killed Billy and Billie Jean. And in the truck bed are three suspiciously full trash bags.

Carefully, with latex-gloved hands, Lott and Hannon slice them open.

To their surprise, inside the bags they find reams of

shredded documents. None of them are readable, but they all appear to be printed emails.

"Potter's got enough confetti for a ticker-tape parade," says Hannon. "Think any of this might be relevant to the case?"

Lott answers, "Based on what I saw this afternoon? Barbara has a history of trying to destroy sensitive pages. So, yes, I have a hunch they're relevant. Let's get 'em to the lab, see if they can't start putting 'em back together."

"But that could take weeks," Hannon says. "Months. If it's even possible at all."

"We're hunting a cold-blooded killer, Mike. We'll tell 'em to pick up the pace."

CHAPTER 27

SPECIAL AGENTS SCOTT LOTT and Mike Hannon guide Buddy Potter into the chief deputy's office for questioning. Like Jamie Curd before him, he takes a seat in the plush leather armchair against the back wall. Lott and Hannon sit across from him on either side.

Unlike Jamie, Buddy's wrists are handcuffed in front of him.

Lott shoots daggers at Buddy, letting him stew for a bit before they get started.

Finally the agent asks, "You know why you're here, right?"

Buddy shrugs. Confident. Nonchalant.

"Somebody's told you I'm the one who killed somebody."

Hannon asks plainly, "Did you? You can be the one to tell us the truth."

Buddy shakes his head. "I'm not gonna tell you I did somethin' I didn't do."

"We don't *think* you killed them," Lott says. "We *know* you killed them, okay?"

"I did not kill Billy Payne and Billie Jean Hayworth. Like my wife told y'all, we heard about it on the news."

"You didn't shoot Billy in the face? Then slit his throat with your bowie knife while he was still gaspin' for his last few breaths? You didn't shoot Billie Jean in the face, too? While she was clutchin' her newborn son, screamin' and cryin' and beggin' for her life?"

"Nope."

"You didn't kill them," says Hannon, "out of revenge for the way they were treatin' your daughter? You didn't kill them to keep Jenelle safe, 'cause you were afraid of what they might do to her?"

Buddy shakes his head. Bored and annoyed. "Y'all can ask it as many different ways as you want. I sure didn't *like* Billy and Billie Jean. But I didn't kill them."

"All right," replies Lott. "Let me ask you something else then, Mr. Potter. What did you say to Jamie Curd on the phone last night?"

Buddy blinks a few times. Then a few times more.

"Come again?"

"Yesterday evening, Jamie placed a telephone call to your home. He spoke briefly with your wife. Then he spoke to you. I'd like to know what you told him."

"I . . . can't remember it exactly."

Hannon takes out a few sheets of paper from a file. "Maybe we can refresh your memory. According to our transcript, Jamie said to you, 'You got rid of everything from Billy's, didn't you?' You said, 'Uh-huh.' What did you mean by that?"

Buddy sags in his seat. He licks his lips.

In an instant, his demeanor has entirely shifted from defiant to that of a very guilty man. But he's also completely clammed up.

Lott asks, "Mr. Potter, are you a cold-blooded killer? Or protector of your family?"

"I'm protector of my family. But I did not do this."

Lott continues, "I believe you were sick and tired of the most precious person in your life being attacked and harassed. Constantly. I know that, okay? I know how you must have felt."

Buddy stares off into the distance.

Then he starts to break down.

"Ever since all this crap started," he says, "I've had my life threatened! My wife has been threatened! They— they've threatened to take Jenelle, cut her head off! Murder her!" The brawny former Marine starts choking back emotion.

Seizing on the momentum, Hannon says, "In your mind, you had no other choice."

Lott says, "You *had* to kill them, Buddy. To protect Jenelle. You had to."

Buddy lifts his cuffed wrists and buries his face in his hands.

The agents wait. Eagerly. But Buddy still won't outright confess.

Their questioning continues like this for quite some time. They come at Buddy from all angles, prodding him again and again to admit his participation in the murders.

And yet he won't.

To anyone watching the interrogation, Buddy's fear, remorse, and guilt are obvious. Along with Jamie's testimony, the matching-caliber bullets found in Buddy's truck, and his admission to having been at the crime scene, it's inconceivable that any jury in the state would let Buddy walk.

Still, Lott and Hannon want an absolutely airtight case. They want a confession.

After a few solid hours of dancing around in circles, Lott gets an idea.

He hands Buddy a telephone and asks him to dial.

"Hello?" says a woman on the other end.

"Barbara?" mutters Buddy. "Before you find out from somebody else . . . I want you to know . . . I was involved in it. I did it. I didn't want you two to be afraid no more."

Barbara lets out a long breath that almost sounds like a whistle.

"Buddy, you're really not yourself right now. You need to think about it more."

"No, Barbara. I *have* thought about it."

"Well, I don't understand what you're even talkin' about," she says, sounding awfully unemotional for a woman whose husband just confessed to two homicides. "You were here at home with me all night! You can tell 'em that if you want. I saw you."

Lott and Hannon exchange a look. Is Barbara suggesting she'll lie for Buddy and provide him an alibi? Does that mean she already *knew* he'd killed Billy and Billie Jean? Could *she* have been involved in the murders as well?

"Yeah, I know but...listen to me, Barb. I just said I did it. It is what it is."

Buddy ends the call and, tail between his legs, hands the receiver back to Lott. He might have managed to avoid confessing directly to his interrogators. But from the slump of his shoulders, it's clear he understands that his fate is sealed.

"What I still wanna know is," Lott says, "how'd you get so much nonsense in your head in the first place? Jenelle and the victims were squabbling online, sure. But that's all it was. We've seen no evidence of any real-life threats made against her or you or your wife. None. Where'd you get all that crap, Potter?"

But Buddy just grumbles, "I'm done talkin'."

CHAPTER 28

Eight months later

IT'S A CRISP AUTUMN day in 2012 when Tennessee assistant district attorney general Dennis Brooks, a senior prosecutor with fourteen years' experience, is assigned the most complex, high-profile, utterly bizarre double-homicide case of his career.

Brooks recalls vividly the local and national media attention the heart-wrenching murders of Billy Payne and Billie Jean Hayworth received earlier in the year. Two vibrant new parents, executed in their own home, one literally holding their infant in her arms—all supposedly because they had unfriended a woman on Facebook?

At least, that was the sensational narrative the press ran with. Was it true?

Brooks has a hunch there's more to the story. First, he'll have to establish a complete timeline and theory of the crimes, and then decide what charges to file against whom—and, most important, what to argue at trial to secure convictions.

Brooks clears off the mahogany desk in his book-lined office, loosens his tie, and cracks open the banker's box that contains all the relevant case materials. Crime scene photos. Autopsy results. Forensic lab reports. Police interrogation notes.

There are reams of documents to sift through, but the case against Buddy Potter and Jamie Curd seems cut-and-dried. The evidence against them is overwhelming. Both men have checkered histories with the victims. Ballistics tests also matched markings on the bullet that killed Billy with similar identifying markings on loose rounds found in Buddy's truck. And just in case the jury still has any doubts, both men are on tape confessing— Buddy to his wife, Jamie to investigators.

But for Brooks, a few things aren't adding up.

First, toward the end of his interrogation, Jamie casually asks investigators the whereabouts of someone named "Chris," who worked for the CIA. Then, on the phone with Jamie, Barbara mentions receiving an email from a Chris as well. Who could they possibly have been referring to? How, if at all, does this mystery man fit into the case?

Second, during Buddy's police interview, he speaks of wanting to protect Jenelle from murder at the hands of Billy and Billie Jean. But the victims were frazzled new parents with no history of violence, who only wanted to be left alone. Where did Buddy get such vile, paranoid ideas?

It doesn't take long for Brooks to get his answers.

At the bottom of the banker's box, he finds a thumb drive. On it is half a gigabyte of Facebook and Topix posts. Copies of hundreds of text messages. And lots and lots of emails. Nearly a thousand in all. Many were pulled from the computers seized at the Potter house, and some were painstakingly reconstructed by the crime lab from the trash bags of shredded documents found in Buddy's pickup.

Brooks plugs in the drive and starts going through this mountain of correspondence between Jenelle, Jamie, Barbara, and "Chris."

What he reads is horrifying—but incredibly illuminating.

Brooks notes that Chris was the one who initiated contact with Barbara and Jamie, and that he was the source of the most outlandish claims—that Billy was in a drug gang, that he was plotting to kill Jenelle and hurt her family—for which there is zero evidence.

Chris's emails are incendiary, claiming to Barbara that Jamie said he was willing to commit murder on Jenelle's behalf, while convincing Jamie that Jenelle might commit suicide if her tormentors weren't stopped. Chris boasts of his own past covert operations and assassinations, and muses about taking out Billy and Billie Jean himself. And he encourages Barbara to bring Jamie and Buddy together to plan and carry out the murder.

Brooks thinks whoever the hell this Chris guy is, *he*

ought to be on trial, too. *What kind of CIA agent would do all this?*

The answer, of course, is obvious.

Despite what the Potters and Jamie Curd seem to believe, Chris isn't a real CIA agent at all.

Not a chance.

Like most people, Brooks doesn't really know much about the Central Intelligence Agency beyond what he's seen in spy movies. But he's pretty damn sure no actual CIA agent would spend months obsessing over a silly social media feud among some melodramatic young people in rural Tennessee.

No actual CIA agent would write literally hundreds of detailed, delusional, inflammatory emails about it.

No actual CIA agent would send anyone a "highly classified photograph" of himself wearing a black shirt and a badge as a way of proving his identity.

No actual CIA agent would share fantasies about killing innocent people.

No actual CIA agent would dupe civilians into committing murder.

For Brooks, the question now becomes: Who's the *real* Chris?

There are multiple candidates, but in his mind, only one of them fits the bill.

Jenelle Potter.

Dennis Brooks soon comes to the conclusion that Jenelle, consumed by her unrequited love for Billy and her intense jealousy of Billie Jean, created the persona of "Chris" to manipulate her boyfriend and parents into murdering the couple.

Brooks knows how his theory must sound.

Jenelle clearly operates on a severely stunted emotional and intellectual level. Could she really have convincingly impersonated a government official for a year and a half and tricked three adults into taking the lives of two others?

Yes, Brooks believes. She could have.

Indeed, rereading the emails through this new lens, Brooks is struck by "Chris's" obsession with Jenelle's thoughts and feelings. For an allegedly long-lost friend living hundreds of miles away, Chris seems quite familiar with Jenelle's deepest fears and insecurities, and heaps praise on her constantly. He also seems to know exactly how to manipulate Barbara and Jamie to get the reactions from them he wants. And notably, Chris even uses many of the same expressions and makes many of the same spelling and grammar errors that Jenelle does in her own emails.

And if Jenelle really has been posing as "Chris" this whole time, Brooks feels strongly that she and Barbara both should face the consequences.

But now the question is, how in the world can he possibly *prove* it?

CHAPTER 29

June 6, 2013

MRS. POTTER, MISS POTTER, thank y'all both again for doing this. I know it's a little inconvenient, but it should really help us out."

Chief Deputy Joe Woodard of the Johnson County Sheriff's Department leads Barbara and Jenelle Potter down a long, fluorescent-lighted hallway.

"We'd write out the Holy Bible for y'all," Barbara huffs, "if it would help you catch these sick people. What's inconvenient is everything they're doin' to *us!*"

The Potter women have claimed that in the ramp-up to Buddy's and Jamie's murder trials, which are scheduled for the fall, they've begun facing *new* acts of harassment and some acts of minor but vindictive home vandalism. Woodard has invited them down to the station to type up their accounts in their own words, which he explains will greatly aid in his department's investigation.

The three arrive at the open doorway of Woodard's

empty private office. He folds his hands on his belly, protruding over his gun and utility belt, and smiles.

"Hopefully this is all we'll need. In here, please, ladies."

Over the next hour, Barbara and Jenelle take turns sitting behind Chief Deputy Woodard's computer typing out lengthy, detailed witness statements, while Woodard watches from an armchair against the back wall.

"These are just great," he says, skimming their finished work on his screen. "A lot of real helpful leads here. We'll get right on 'em." Jenelle and Barbara start to leave. "Miss Potter, before you go, can I ask your help with one more little thing? I understand you've also been the victim of some online hacking in the past, ain't that right?"

"You mean my Facebook? Yeah. A ton."

"Well, to help us know if it happens again, can you take a gander at some of this stuff we pulled from your account and tell me if you're the one who actually wrote it?"

Jenelle exchanges a slightly wary look with her mother, but she agrees.

Woodard gives her a pen and printout with various passages cut and pasted from her Facebook profile, including the ABOUT ME section and a handful of other posts. Jenelle reads the passages carefully. She makes a check next to nearly all of them.

"I can't remember these two. But the rest...yeah, I wrote 'em."

"Fantastic," Woodard says with a clap of his hands. "We'll be in touch real soon."

The chief deputy escorts Jenelle and Barbara out of the building.

Then he hustles back to his office and sits down at his computer.

Assistant District Attorney General Dennis Brooks is in his office, on the phone, when an alert pops up on his screen that he's received a new email—from Johnson County Sheriff's Department chief deputy Joe Woodard.

Brooks pumps his fist in victory. "Hank, I gotta call you back."

Attached to Woodard's email is the long, rambling witness statement Jenelle Potter has just written. Also attached is a scanned copy of multiple passages from her Facebook profile that she verified she wrote herself.

Brooks can scarcely contain his excitement as he forwards the email to Dr. Robert Leonard, a professor of forensic linguistics at Hofstra University in New York, with whom he's been in frequent contact over the last several months.

The modern digital equivalent of a handwriting expert, Dr. Leonard specializes in developing advanced computer algorithms that analyze a host of syntactic and lexical factors in order to establish "authorship identification" of unknown textual sources.

Simply put, Brooks is hoping the professor will be able

to verify—and then testify—that the emails from "Chris" (as well as the derogatory Topix message board posts from various pseudonyms) were all actually penned by Jenelle.

But in order to do so, Dr. Leonard had some very stringent requirements. For one, he needed a completely original, stand-alone "K doc" (aka a document *known* to have been written by the suspect) to compare with the "Q docs" (aka the emails and message threads in *question*). Like the Q docs, the K doc had to be typed, not handwritten. It had to have been drafted by the suspect completely unassisted, not under duress, and in her own voice. And an independent observer had to be watching the entire time to ensure its authenticity.

For a while, Brooks was stumped. How in the world could he convince Jenelle to do something like that? But after he learned that the Potter women were claiming renewed harassment, it hit him. He enlisted the help of Chief Deputy Woodard, and their plan worked like a charm.

A few weeks later, Brooks receives a fateful call from Dr. Leonard.

The professor informs him that, with an extremely high degree of scientific certainty, *both the Topix posts and the emails from "Chris" were indeed written by Jenelle.*

It confirms Brooks's theory. But part of him still can't believe it—and doesn't know if he can convince a jury—until a week later when he receives additional evidence from the Tennessee Bureau of Investigation.

At the DA's request, the TBI's Department of Digital

Forensics conducted further technical analysis of the many emails exchanged between Jenelle, Barbara, Jamie, and "Chris," focusing primarily on determining the Internet Protocol addresses from which they were sent (that is, the unique string of numbers and letters that identifies a computer's location when it's connected to the web). It turned out that although Chris was presumably emailing from his office at CIA headquarters in Langley, Virginia—or wherever his international jet-setting secret-agent life took him—every single one of his emails originated from the same IP address in Mountain City: Jenelle Potter's personal computer.

Linguistically and digitally, Brooks now has his proof.

Chris is Jenelle.

Jenelle is Chris.

She's also Matt and Kelly and Dan and Mike, for that matter.

The nasty online smear campaign against Billy Payne and Billie Jean Hayworth was all Jenelle's doing.

So was the sick scheme to manipulate her parents and boyfriend.

Buddy pulled the trigger.

Jamie kept watch.

Barbara encouraged it.

But the true monster in all of this was Jenelle Potter.

CHAPTER 30

May 2015

IT SOUNDED LIKE SUCH a good idea at the time.

A swing for the fences, sure. But a bold and gallant grasp at justice.

Now, driving to the courthouse for the first day of Jenelle and Barbara Potter's joint murder trial, prosecutor Dennis Brooks is having some second thoughts.

At least there's some comfort in knowing that, no matter what happens, Jamie will be spending decades in prison and Buddy will die there. Buddy's open-and-shut case wrapped up about eighteen months ago, with Brooks successfully securing a double life sentence. Jamie took a plea deal and accepted twenty-five years.

But for a dedicated prosecutor like Brooks, partial justice isn't good enough.

Still, he's wondering whether he was right to charge both women with conspiracy to commit first-degree murder as well as *actual* first-degree murder.

The former charge only requires that a defendant be found to have "solicited, directed, aided or attempted to aid" someone in the commission of a homicide, which Brooks is supremely confident he'll be able to successfully argue. He can point to dozens of emails in which Barbara, Jamie Curd, and "Chris" talk openly and excitedly about killing Billy Payne and Billie Jean Hayworth and egg one another on to do so. That's about as clear a case of criminal conspiracy as you can get.

It's the latter charge that Brooks is concerned about.

Jenelle and Barbara didn't fire the gun that killed Billy and Billie Jean. They didn't hold the knife that slit Billy's throat. They didn't drive with Buddy Potter to Paw Bill's house or stand guard outside, like Jamie. On the night of the murders, neither woman was anywhere *near* the crime scene. In fact, it's possible they were fast asleep.

Will a jury still be willing to convict them of first-degree murder? If not, Brooks worries, will they throw out the entire case to punish the DA's office for overreach?

He tries to shake any lingering doubts from his mind as he climbs the stone steps of the stately county courthouse. After many months of trial delays, Brooks is finally delivering his opening statement. And he knows he only gets one shot at making a compelling first impression.

"All rise!" bellows the bailiff. "This court is now in session, the Honorable Judge Jon Kerry Blackwood presiding."

The bald, bookish, bespectacled old judge trundles to his seat on the bench and instructs the courtroom to be seated. With no new motions or other administrative matters to deal with, he invites the prosecution to give its remarks.

Brooks rises, buttons his suit jacket, and strides toward the jury box. He glances briefly at the defendants sitting behind him, then takes a deep breath.

"There is nothing in your lives or background that has prepared you to understand the Potter family," he says with quiet forcefulness. "You have never seen anybody like them. The story is very, very simple. It is a story of a manufactured conflict born in the mind of a very bored, lonely, thirty-year-old woman. Everything that happened...happened as the direct result of Jenelle Potter's deeply twisted actions."

Brooks shows the jury crime scene photos of Billy and Billie Jean lying dead in pools of their own blood. To accompany them, he reads selections from various Topix posts in which Jenelle, writing under different fake names, professes her deep-rooted hatred of the victims and her desire that they and their "bastard baby...die die die!" Then Brooks reads snippets from various emails in which Jenelle, writing as Chris, spurs her boyfriend and mother to make her homicidal fantasies a reality.

Pointing now to Jenelle and Barbara, Brooks warns that thanks to these two, the jury is in for the wildest, craziest, most unbelievable story they've ever heard in their lives. But every word of it is true. And there are piles of evidence to prove it.

Brooks ends his opening statement and takes his seat.

Over the course of his career, he's learned that trying to read jurors' faces is about as accurate as trying to read tea leaves. Nonetheless, he takes the uniform look of shock and horror on all twelve faces as a very good sign.

Until the lead defense attorney rises and gives *his* opening statement.

Cameron Hyder is Dennis Brooks's polar opposite in almost every way. Where the middle-aged Brooks can be staid and avuncular, Hyder is young, vibrant, handsome, and dynamic. His slim designer suit is custom-made. His hair is perfectly gelled. His gold cuff links, embossed with his initials, sparkle under the courtroom lights.

And his opening statement brims with fire and passion.

Hyder argues that Jenelle and Barbara Potter are the real victims here. That the two women fell prey to the hacking and scheming of a demented Jamie Curd. Jealous that Jenelle loved Billy more than she loved him, Jamie was the one who convinced Barbara and Buddy to help him murder his romantic rival so he could have their daughter all to himself.

Hyder also argues that his clients are now being victimized yet again—this time by an overzealous prosecutor. The state's computer evidence is faulty. Its linguistic "expert" is a total quack. And its central theory that Jenelle—a scared, sheltered young woman with the mental acuity of a fifth grader—is some kind of criminal mastermind? Well, that's just utterly absurd.

Brooks hates to admit it—and definitely tries not to show it—but he finds Hyder's opening statement alarmingly sharp and compelling.

Maybe the trial is going to be even tougher than he imagined.

CHAPTER 31

A FEW DAYS LATER, Dennis Brooks is feeling like a kid awaiting Christmas morning.

Not because the trial is going well, although he believes that it is.

Brooks has a major surprise in store for the jury. Something he was careful not to reveal in his opening statement, or any subsequent remarks. Something the defense team hasn't mentioned, either.

But Brooks is positive it's going to blow the damn roof off the place.

Currently, he's wrapping up his questioning of Tennessee Bureau of Investigation special agent Scott Lott, the lead state investigator in the criminal case.

Specifically, Brooks is asking, "When you first learned about Chris, was it important to you to figure out if such a person existed?"

"Yes, it was."

"Did you actually take some steps to contact the CIA and see if you could find a Chris who worked there?"

"I did. Eventually."

"But you couldn't find him?"

"No, sir."

Brooks pauses. "You found...*a* Chris, though, didn't you?"

"Yes, sir. After some digging, I did."

"And he's here today. Ain't he?"

"Yes, sir. He is."

Confused murmurs emanate from the gallery.

Brooks turns to Judge Blackwood. With a dramatic flourish he proclaims, "Your Honor, the state calls Chris Tjaden to the stand!"

The murmurs turn to gasps as a trim Caucasian man in his midthirties with buzzed, dark-brown hair approaches the bench to be sworn in.

"Your Honor, what is the meaning of this?!" demands defense attorney Cameron Hyder, shooting to his feet. "The prosecution spent the last two days questioning a so-called expert who tried—and failed—to convince us that 'Chris' was actually the alter ego of one of my clients. Now they want us to believe he's real after all?"

Judge Blackwood crosses his arms. "I'm as curious as you are, Counsel," he says, and lets Brooks question his surprise witness as Hyder simmers.

"Can you please state your name, occupation, and

place of residence for the record?" Brooks asks the man on the witness stand.

"Christopher Tjaden. I'm a police officer in New Castle County, Delaware."

"Do you know either of the defendants, Mr. Tjaden?"

"I do. Me and Jenelle went to high school together in Pennsylvania."

"And how would you describe your relationship?"

"Honestly? We didn't have one. I would say hello to her in the hall sometimes, but that's about it. She was one of those kids who was very strange. She always had issues. She was always complaining about a problem with somebody."

"When was the last time you had any contact with Miss Potter?"

"High school graduation. Seventeen years ago. She Facebooked me a while ago, but I never accepted her friend request."

Brooks shows Tjaden a photo of a man wearing a black collared shirt with a gold badge pinned to his chest. It's the "classified" photo that "Chris" first emailed to Barbara a few years ago to convince her he was who he claimed to be.

"Is this you, Mr. Tjaden?"

"Yep. That used to be my public Facebook profile picture, actually."

"So this isn't a top secret portrait of a covert intelligence agent?"

Chris chuckles. "Top secret? My mom took it with her cell phone."

"Mr. Tjaden, are you currently, or have you ever been, employed by the Central Intelligence Agency in any capacity?"

"The CIA? Are you serious? No, sir."

"Have you ever emailed either Barbara Potter or Jamie Curd anytime in the past few years?"

"I've never emailed with either of them in my entire life."

Brooks rests his hands on his hips. "One final question, Mr. Tjaden. If you aren't friends with either of the defendants...if you've never been in email contact with them...if you're not a real CIA agent...how did you possibly get tangled up in this mess?"

Hyder angrily rises. "Objection. Calls for speculation."

"I'll allow it," responds Judge Blackwood.

Tjaden thinks for a moment. "I've been wondering that from the moment Special Agent Lott over there tracked me down and knocked on my door. I think Jenelle used to have a crush on me, you know? Years later, when she was looking for a name for her crazy plot and a picture of a guy with a badge, she picked me. Why? I'll never know."

Brooks thanks Tjaden and takes his seat. Judge Blackwood gives Hyder the chance to cross-examine the witness, but the lawyer declines. Brooks doesn't blame him. Every second Tjaden stays on the stand, Jenelle looks nuttier and nuttier.

Brooks is confident he's convinced the jury beyond a reasonable doubt that "Chris" the CIA agent was really Jenelle all along.

But will he be able to convince them that she and her mother are guilty of murder?

CHAPTER 32

GLIMPSING BILLY PAYNE'S FATHER, Paw Bill, in the gallery, along with Billy's sister, Tracy Greenwell, and Billie Jean Hayworth's friend Lindsey Thomas, prosecutor Dennis Brooks feels the weight of his responsibility even more.

The family and friends of the victims are counting on him to deliver justice.

Taking a moment to settle his nerves, he rises and delivers his closing statement, ending the trial the same way he started it—with a clear recitation of the facts and a simple, compelling theory that ties them all together.

Brooks knows the jury has been inundated with an enormous number of confusing and contradictory claims, so he has worked hard to highlight only what he believes are the most crucial arguments and most pertinent pieces of evidence.

Jenelle Potter, he tells them, is a troubled, envious, devious young woman.

She regularly hurled pseudonymous online insults at her perceived rivals to make herself feel better. When that didn't work, she created a fictitious character who perfectly exploited her parents' fears and her boyfriend's devotion, and over the course of many months, managed to persuade them to commit murder. She may not be very bright, but Jenelle Potter is a diabolical genius— and a ruthless killer.

Barbara Potter, Brooks argues, is no angel, either.

Yes, she was manipulated by her daughter. But the many violent threats she directed against Billy and Billie Jean were completely her own. Barbara was the one who invited Jamie Curd over on the night of the murders to "fix the family computer," when really it was to get him together with her husband so they could conspire. Remember how blasé she was when Buddy Potter called to confess his crimes, Brooks reminds jurors, and how she immediately offered to provide him a fake alibi? Even if Barbara erroneously believed she was protecting her daughter, she's nevertheless as guilty of murder as Buddy and Jamie are.

Brooks concludes with a simple thought experiment.

Given everything they now know about the case, he asks the jury to close their eyes and imagine whether Billy and Billie Jean would still have been killed if they'd never had the misfortune to cross paths with Jenelle and

Barbara. The answer will make clear whether the two Potter women were simply bystanders caught up in a tragedy—or the actual instigators.

"If you can't imagine these crimes happening without them," Brooks says, "then you know in your heart what your verdict must be. You have before you the two people most responsible for Billy Payne and Billie Jean Hayworth lying there dead, and their baby being left without his parents." Solemnly, Brooks ends with, "We ask you to bring justice for these deaths. Thank you."

The court adjourns, and Brooks retreats to a quiet corner of the DA's office to try to stay busy and keep his mind occupied while the jury deliberates. Waiting for a verdict is always torture, especially in such a high-profile, high-stakes case.

He immediately throws himself back into the many other routine cases he'd been neglecting in recent months as the Potter trial took over his life. There's comfort in reviewing case files for simple burglaries, drug deals, and DUIs again. There are no reams of graphic emails to slog through. No false identities to untangle. No arcane digital or forensic linguistic terminology to master. No camera crews camped out in front of the courthouse to dodge. No murdered parents and orphaned child to fight for.

At the same time, however, Brooks is agitated. When the first day of deliberations ends with no verdict, he feels a pit open up in his stomach. *What the hell is taking the jury so long to decide?*

Is there disagreement among the jurors?

Are they struggling to find a consensus on the multiple charges?

Are they going to let Jenelle and Barbara walk free?

The next morning, after a sleepless night, Brooks gets even more concerning news.

The jury has requested a laptop to rewatch certain suspect interviews.

Of all the material they could have asked for, Brooks wonders, *why the interrogation tapes? Was the rest of the evidence really not enough?*

Finally, after lunch, word begins to spread that the jury has reached a verdict.

Judge Blackwood gavels the court back into session. The twelve stone-faced jurors return to the jury box. Jenelle, Barbara, and their attorney all stand.

"Count one," reads the foreperson, "we the jury find the defendant Barbara Mae Potter guilty of first-degree murder. Count two, we the jury find the defendant Barbara Mae Potter guilty of conspiracy to commit first-degree murder."

Wails of shock and elation echo throughout the courtroom.

"Order!" Judge Blackwood cries. "Or I'll have you all removed."

Brooks is still holding his breath. It's not over yet.

The foreperson continues, "Count one, we the jury find the defendant Jenelle Leigh Potter guilty of first-degree murder. Count two, we the jury find the defendant Jenelle Leigh Potter guilty of conspiracy to commit first-degree murder."

Only now does Brooks let himself exhale—and let his tears flow freely—as gasps of shock and shouts of triumph erupt throughout the courtroom.

He is so overcome, he almost doesn't hear Judge Blackwood gavel his court back to order, then immediately hand down life sentences to both Barbara and Jenelle.

Brooks slumps in his seat, exhausted but victorious.

He has just won the most difficult and wacko trial of his career.

He has delivered justice to two innocent people, brand-new parents killed simply for befriending a disturbed, delusional young woman with an unrequited crush—and a deadly manipulative streak. Worse, the victims might still be alive were it not for the power of social media to blur the line between reality and fantasy.

Brooks knows this stranger-than-fiction case has shaken this quiet, close-knit community to its core. It's one that the people of Mountain City—and all across the world—will be talking about for years to come.

In books. On television.

And yes, of course, all across social media.

ABOUT THE AUTHORS

James Patterson is the world's bestselling author and most trusted storyteller. He has created many enduring fictional characters and series, including Alex Cross, the Women's Murder Club, Michael Bennett, Maximum Ride, Middle School, and I Funny. Among his notable literary collaborations are *The President Is Missing,* with President Bill Clinton, and the Max Einstein series, produced in partnership with the Albert Einstein Estate. Patterson's writing career is characterized by a single mission: to prove that there is no such thing as a person who "doesn't like to read," only people who haven't found the right book. He's given over three million books to schoolkids and the military, donated more than seventy million dollars to support education, and endowed over five thousand college scholarships for teachers. For his prodigious imagination and championship of literacy in America, Patterson was awarded the 2019 National Humanities Medal. The National Book Foundation presented him with the Literarian Award for Outstanding Service to the American Literary Community, and he is also the recipient of an Edgar Award and nine Emmy Awards. He lives in Florida with his family.

Andrew Bourelle is the author of the novel *Heavy Metal* and coauthor with James Patterson of *Texas Ranger* and *Texas Outlaw*. His short stories have been published widely in literary magazines and fiction anthologies, including *The Best American Mystery Stories*.

Max DiLallo is a novelist, playwright, and screenwriter. He lives in Los Angeles.